How to Buy a Company

How to Buy a Company

Edited by

THOMAS R. ANGEAR and
JOHN DEWHURST

Published in association with the Institute of Directors

DIRECTOR BOOKS

Published by Director Books,
an imprint of Fitzwilliam Publishing Limited,
Simon & Schuster International Group,
Fitzwilliam House, 32 Trumpington Street,
Cambridge CB2 1QY, England

First published 1989

British Library Cataloguing in Publication Data

How to buy a company
1. Great Britain. Companies. Acquisition.
Management aspects
I. Angear, Thomas R.   II. Dewhurst, John
III. Institute of Directors
658.1'6

ISBN 1-870555-12-0

Designed by Geoff Green
Typeset by Quorn Selective Repro Ltd

Printed in Great Britain by A. Wheaton & Co., Ltd., Exeter

To Patricia and Betty

Contents

The contributors   xi

Introduction Thomas R. Angear and John Dewhurst   xv

1   Defining the acquisition strategy *Ron Sandler*   1
    Introduction   1
    The requirement for an acquisition strategy   2
    Establishing the strategic vision   5
    Creating value through acquisitions   8
    Setting screening criteria   12
    Practical considerations in defining acquisition strategies   13

2   Finding suitable businesses
    Michael J. D. Stallibrass   16
    Introduction   16
    Sources of acquisition opportunities   17
    The business broker   21
    M & A consultants   22
    The financial adviser   23
    Fees   23
    Managing the search process   24
    Cross-border acquisitions   26
    Conclusion   27

3   Methods of financial valuation *John Allday*   29
    Introduction   29
    The earnings basis of valuation   30
    The assets basis of valuation   35
    Other bases of valuation   37
    Acquisition and merger accounting   39
    Financing acquisitions   42

4   Evaluating companies for acquisition
    Jonathan F. Taylor and John Dewhurst   47
    Introduction   47
    The Booker story   48
      Introduction   48
      Sources of acquisitions   49
    Synergy, strategy and simplicity   50
      Adding value   50
      Cashflow – the acid test   52
    The ICI experience   54
      Introduction   54
      Features of large acquisitions   55
    Strategic review   56
      The auction process   56
      Due diligence procedures   57
      Decision day   59

5   Negotiating the deal *David Michaels*   61
    Introduction   61
    The negotiating process   62
    Price parameters and techniques   66
    Strategies   68
    Completion   71
    Conclusion   72

6   Legal aspects of acquisitions *Ian F. Elder*   73
    Scope   73
    Legal status of the target   73
    The legal status of the seller   74
    Purchase of a business   74
    Jurisdictions   75
    Competition and other regulatory approvals   75
    Heads of Agreement/Letters of Intent   76
    Advisers   76
    Quoted and unquoted companies   77
    The price   78
    The Agreement   79
    Warranties   80
    The Disclosure Letter   82
    Limitations on warranties   83
    Indemnification   83
    The company's management   83
    Final thoughts   84

7   Pensions and incentive arrangements
    E. M. Belmont   85
    Pensions   85
        Introduction   85
        What is a pension scheme?   85
        Pot of gold or can of worms?   89
        The pension clause of the sale agreement   92
        Strategy   95
        Conclusion   97
    Incentive arrangements   98
        Why have incentive schemes?   98
        Choosing the right kind of scheme   101
        Bringing the new company into your existing
        incentive schemes   102
        What if your target company already has a
        share scheme?   103
        Some final points to consider   104
        Acknowledgement   106

8   The importance of public relations
    Martin Wray   107
    Introduction   107
    When and where to begin PR   107
    The three phases of PR   108
    Announcement day   114
    The contested bid   116
    External PR advice   117
    Conclusion   118

9   Post-acquisition management *Richard Wood*   120
    Introduction   120
    The pre-implementation phase   121
    The announcement   122
    Post-acquisition managerial control   123
    The honeymoon period   124
    Communications   125
    The post-acquisition management plan   126
    Conclusion   131
    References   131

10 Minimising the risk factor in acquisitions
    Thomas R. Angear   132
    Horizontal, vertical and conglomerate acquisitions   132
    Geographical and psychological distance   133
    Common acquisition mistakes   134

Acquisition errors in the USA   136
The concept of relatedness   136
The human factor in acquisitions   138
The search for added value   139
Guidelines for success in cross-border acquisitions   140
References   142

Appendix A   Sources of information   143

Appendix B   Due diligence requirements   145

*Appendix C   Extract from the City Code on Takeovers
and Mergers*   167

*Appendix D   Preliminary information on
target companies*   169

Index   177

The contributors

John Allday qualified as a chartered accountant in 1963 and became a partner in Ernst & Whinney in 1975. For the past thirteen years he has specialised in the valuation of unquoted shares and business undertakings, and has wide experience of valuation principles and theory adopted throughout Europe, the USA and the Middle East. He has experience of acting as an expert in arbitration proceedings and is continually involved in negotiations relating to the purchase and sale of businesses. He is head of the specialist valuation section of Ernst & Whinney's Corporate Finance Department in London.

Thomas Angear is Managing Director of Trabel Associates Limited and M & A International in London. He graduated from Nottingham University with an honours degree in Industrial Economics and was awarded a Harkness Fellowship for two years' travel and study in the USA. After completing a Master of Business Administration degree at Cornell University's Johnson Graduate School of Management, he spent eight years in marketing management with Lever Brothers and Warner-Lambert, followed by three years as Managing Director of McAlley Associates, a corporate strategy consultancy. He has been involved with international mergers and acquisitions since 1973, forming his own consultancy in 1978, and has initiated over 100 successful transactions during this period. He is a regular contributor to professional journals and a guest speaker at international management conferences. Thomas Angear is a founder director of Unicom Electronics Limited and is also Chairman of Omicron Management Software Limited.

E. M. Belmont is an honours graduate of Oxford University and a Fellow of the Institute of Actuaries. He has been involved in pensions work for seventeen years, the last nine of which have been with a firm of actuarial consultants, Buck Paterson Consultants Limited. In 1987, he opened the company's new Leeds office and holds the position of Divisional Director. He has lectured and written various articles on the pensions aspects of mergers and acquisitions. Ted Belmont describes himself as a believer in the role of the actuary as a practical man not an obscure theoretician.

John Dewhurst is Acquisitions Manager of ICI PLC. He graduated from the London School of Economics with an honours degree in Economics in 1963. In the same year he joined British Nylon Spinners which was subsequently taken over by ICI. He has held a number of positions in various parts of ICI including nearly five years as General Manager of a joint-venture company in Spain. In 1984 he joined the Acquisitions Team and in 1987 was appointed to his present post. Since the establishment of this team, ICI has completed over 150 acquisitions and divestments. He is a regular speaker at national and international conferences on practical matters relating to acquisitions.

Ian Elder is a solicitor, qualified in both England and Scotland, with Messrs Allen & Overy. He attended St Andrews University, where he obtained an MA, and Edinburgh University, where he obtained an LLB. From 1974 to 1977, he was with the well-known firm of Edinburgh solicitors, Messrs Dundas & Wilson, as an Apprentice and as an Assistant Solicitor. He joined the Legal Department of Imperial Chemical Industries PLC in 1978, in which he became a senior member, working on a wide range of commercial and financial transactions. He was the coordinating lawyer for ICI in one of its largest acquisitions, namely the purchase in 1986 of the American paint company Glidden, from Hanson. He left ICI in 1987 to join Allen & Overy.

David Michaels established and is Chairman of The Guidehouse Group Plc in 1980 which went on the USM in August 1987. The activities of the Group are issuing house, stockbroker, lending institution, insurance broking, recruitment and advertising. He is also a director of a number of companies including Hornby Group plc, W. H. Allen and Co. plc, Alliance Property and Construction plc and the Lachmead Group plc.

His previous career was diverse. He qualified as a statistician at University College London and worked as a consultant statistician at University College Hospital. A range of other activities followed a business degree with spells at Freemans Limited, GEC and Logica, followed by eight years at N. M. Rothschild and Sons, where he headed the mergers and acquisitions activity. He has had a number of articles published on scientific and financial subjects.

Ron Sandler is the Managing Director of OC Sandler Associates, a consultancy which specialises in assisting small and medium-sized companies in developing and implementing expansion strategies.

In his consulting career over the last twelve years, Ron Sandler has specialised in corporate strategy and acquisition work. Prior to founding OC Sandler Associates, he was Senior Vice President of Booz Allen & Hamilton and Managing Director of Booz Allen's UK operations. Previously he was a Vice President and Director of The Boston Consulting Group. Before entering the consulting profession, he was with The Anglo-American Corporation of South Africa.

He holds an MA, in Engineering, from Queens' College, Cambridge and an MBA, with Distinction, from Stanford University.

Michael J. D. Stallibrass is an Executive Director of Shearson Lehman Hutton International, Inc. and Head of their Mergers and Acquisitions Department in London. He has a degree in Natural Sciences from Oxford University. Prior to taking up his current position at Shearson Lehman Hutton he had spent ten years in the Corporate Finance Department of Kleinwort, Benson Limited, latterly as an Assistant Director of that bank.

Jonathan F. Taylor was educated at Winchester College and Corpus Christi College, Oxford (open scholar) BA, MA. Since August 1984 he has been Chief Executive of Booker, an international food and agricultural business with sales of £2,000 million. Mr Taylor joined Booker in 1959. In his early career he was involved in all aspects of Booker's international agribusiness operations, becoming Chairman of its agriculture division in 1976. In 1980 Mr Taylor joined the Board of Booker and moved to New York as President of Ibec Inc., a US corporation in which Booker held a 45 per cent interest and the Rockefeller family 55 per cent. From 1980 to 1984 he was responsible for the management and development of Ibec as a major agribusiness which includes Arbor Acres and Nicholas Turkey, Booker Agriculture International and new investments in farm and forest management as seed genetics in the UK. In mid-1984 Mr Taylor returned to the UK to become Chief Executive of Booker following a takeover bid from The Dee Corporation. He was responsible for the subsequent defence of Booker which culminated in the rejection of the bid in April 1985.

Jonathan Taylor has spoken at a number of conferences and seminars and has contributed several case-studies to the Harvard Business School. He has served as an occasional adviser to the World Bank, the US Agency for International Development and UK Overseas Development Administration. He is a Director of Tate & Lyle PLC.

Richard K. Wood is a Chartered Chemical Engineer, a Fellow of the

Institute of Directors, and a senior business manager with ICI. His career has involved extensive experience in production, marketing, international business management and general management in various senior positions at subsidiary board level.

Throughout his career, he has been directly involved in more than 20 acquisitions, mergers or joint ventures. During the 1980s he was the architect of a progressive diversification strategy which involved five major acquisitions, with expenditure totalling more than £200 million. In this period, he was head or number two negotiator followed by responsibility for various stages of the post-acquisition management, including that of Chief Executive Officer.

Martin Wray, a Cambridge graduate in Modern Languages (Russian and German), spent the first seven years of his career in the Foreign Office, serving in London and Berlin. He joined ICI in 1960, working first on export sales to Eastern Europe and Scandinavia, and then in the corporate East European Department, of which he became Head in 1972. In 1975 he moved to ICI's Trade Affairs Department, first as Head of its UK Government Relations Group, then as Head of the Department. In 1983 he took over the newly-created Public Affairs Department with responsibility for Government and EEC Affairs, media relations, corporate publicity and international trade issues. In this role he had personal responsibility for the communications aspects of the series of major acquisitions in the USA and elsewhere made by ICI over recent years.

Upon retiring from ICI in August 1987, Martin Wray became a freelance consultant on corporate communications issues. He specialises in the provision of discreet, behind-the-scenes counselling to corporate management on UK and EEC Government Relations, the communications aspects of takeover and acquisitions matters, relations with the City and the financial press, and, more generally, in the handling of relationships with the UK media. He is an Associate of City & Corporate Counsel Ltd, a company specialising in the provision of specialist and exclusive service to senior management and their in-house advisers.

Introduction

THOMAS R. ANGEAR and
JOHN DEWHURST

Mergers and acquisitions are headline news. The annual expenditure on takeovers continues to spiral ever upwards. In 1987, total spending in the United Kingdom reached a staggering £27.7 billion involving 1,937 separate transactions, an increase in value on 1986 of just over 10 per cent. Not content with this domestic spending-spree, British companies proceeded to invest a record $31.7 billion in purchasing 262 companies in the USA, an increase of 50 per cent over the previous year. This investment wave continued unabated throughout 1988 in spite of the stock market crash in October 1987. Total spending in the UK increased to £37.6 billion representing 2,241 completed transactions. Investment in the USA remained constant at $31.7 billion although this reflected a larger number of completions – 385 in total, an increase of 47 per cent over 1987. Significantly, British companies also increased their acquisition activity in continental Europe by over 50 per cent, recording 252 transactions with an expenditure of £2.6 billion. The amount of money spent by continental European companies in the UK in 1988 showed a *threefold* increase over 1987 at £5.1 billion, and this trend can be expected to accelerate.

Takeovers also make good newspaper copy because of the highly personalised and often acrimonious nature of contested bid battles where the protagonists argue the merits of their case in the public arena. Until quite recently companies in the United Kingdom have been relatively immune from the threat of foreign invasion, but the highly charged Rowntree/Nestlé/Suchard saga of 1988 resurrected xenophobic feelings not seen since the end of the Second World War. Furthermore, we now have the run-up to 1992 and the truly 'common' market with all that that entails for British companies intending to strengthen their presence by acquisition and joint ventures within the EEC.

And yet, the front-page stories conceal two significant factors which are essential to a more complete understanding of this fascinating and complex industry.

First, the failure rate of acquisitions is very much higher than might be expected. Many years ago Lord Leverhulme was reported to have said, 'One half of all advertising is wasted – but I am not sure which half.' Much the same could be said today about the vast expenditure on mergers and acquisitions with the exception that, in this case, it is rather more easy to identify the 50 per cent that is 'wasted'. Clearly, an industry of this magnitude that can 'guarantee' only a 2:1 chance of success on average requires much more detailed study and analysis.

Secondly, the 'blockbuster' bids obscure the fact that 60 per cent of all acquisitions in the UK have a value of less than £3 million! The industry is obviously a very large iceberg with a highly observable 'tip' and a mass of relatively small transactions hidden from public scrutiny.

The idea for this book arose from the need to address both these important issues in much greater detail. The editors were also aware that earlier publications had tended to adopt a mechanistic approach to the subject, reflecting, in the main, the legal, accounting or academic backgrounds of the authors. We recognised the need for a new publication which would draw upon the collective experiences of several noted industry experts who would contribute both the essential technical information and the benefits of their own personal observations and insight. Just as the editors spend their entire working week either initiating, negotiating, consummating or managing acquisitions, so have all the contributors developed a deep professional understanding of many of the specialist areas of the business. We thank them for their expert advice and for their collective wisdom.

This book is both a reference work – in terms of the technical, legal, accounting and actuarial requirements of the subject matter itself – and, also, a source of advice and recommendations for improved understanding and performance. Its message is directed towards the owners and directors of both public and private companies who wish to expand their businesses by acquisition. It is to be hoped that the reader will personally benefit from the lessons to be learned from the numerous industry failures and avoid the many pitfalls along the road. In addition, two messages should emerge from this publication – the imperative search for *added value* and the critical importance of *post-acquisition management*. If we have succeeded in directing attention to these two key concepts our contribution to the continuing debate on this fascinating subject will have been entirely justified.

Tom Angear
John Dewhurst

Chapter 1

Defining the acquisition strategy

RON SANDLER

Managing Director, OC Sandler Associates

Introduction

The prospect of making an acquisition generates more excitement than any other item on the management agenda. The reasons for this are not hard to find. For some, the excitement comes from the process leading up to acquisition – the selection, stalking and capturing of an unsuspecting quarry. For others, the fascination with acquisition lies with the prospect of the takeover itself – with obtaining control over another business and dealing with the challenges of integration. For all, making an acquisition provides a change of routine and an often welcome diversion from the day-to-day pressures of management.

Not only are managers excited by the prospect of an acquisition. The adrenalin boost that a takeover generates is equally observable in the group of professional advisers to the transaction, perhaps influenced by the success-based fee incentives which have become commonplace. The business press also plays its part in fuelling acquisition interest, devoting a disproportionate amount of space on the financial pages to takeover activity, particularly in the case of hostile bids. The public spotlight under which a management team is placed during an acquisition is far more intense than at any other time in the corporate calendar.

There is little doubt that these factors have contributed to the spectacular growth in acquisition activity, in the UK and elsewhere, in recent years. They are, however, only a small part of the overall picture, and a number of other forces are at work. Structural shifts in the economy, most notably in favour of the service sector, have caused many companies to turn their attention to diversification – and acquisition has many obvious attractions as a vehicle for entry into new business areas. The prolonged strength of the equity markets, notwithstanding the crash of October 1987, has added considerably to the availability of risk capital to fund acquisitions. Yet perhaps the most important factor of all is the increasing stress placed by the financial community on short-term growth in earnings per share.

The pressure that this creates upon management, coupled in the UK with current rules regarding merger accounting, have helped to establish acquisition as a favoured tool for corporate development. Indeed, for many companies, acquisition and corporate development have become synonymous.

Taking all of these factors into account, it is hardly surprising that acquisition activity in the UK has surged to historic levels. In 1987, it is estimated that almost 2,000 UK companies were acquired, with a value of £28 billion. Furthermore, surveys of executives of leading corporations indicate quite clearly that, at least for the foreseeable future, this phenomenon is here to stay and acquisition activity will remain at a high level.

What is more surprising, given this enthusiasm for takeover, is the fact that, more often than not, acquisitions fail to produce the benefits anticipated. A number of studies have been undertaken in recent years, both by academic researchers and management consultants, on the subject of acquisition success. This research has pointed consistently to the conclusion that, on average, for every successful acquisition there are two failures. The reasons underlying this somewhat sobering statistic have been explored from a number of perspectives. Time and again, the diagnosis has pointed to a deficiency in concept rather than poor execution. Put more simply, the underlying acquisition strategy has been faulty. The potential for value creation has not been correctly assessed.

There have, of course, been some spectacular success stories. The track records of corporations such as Hanson Trust and BTR demonstrate that in some organisations acquisition can be an extremely effective means of creating value for shareholders. But for the majority of acquirers, the reality is that the acquisition, more often than not, will fail to produce the expected benefits.

Reduced to fundamentals, acquisitions succeed for one of two reasons: either the acquired assets represent an undervalued bargain, or the resources of the acquirer can be combined with those of the target so as to create value. In today's world, with the widespread dissemination of information, bargains are becoming increasingly scarce. More and more, the success of an acquisition hinges on the potential to create value, either by improving the stand-alone performance of the acquired entity or by creating and exploiting synergies. In the final analysis, this is the essence of acquisition strategy: the ability to identify clearly opportunities for value-creation.

The requirement for an acquisition strategy

It is perhaps self-evident that, given the risks involved, acquisitions require meticulous planning and a sound strategic underpinning. Yet it is none the less true that few companies invest the necessary time and attention to the formulation of coherent and rigorous acquisition strategies. Too often the strategy is a hastily constructed rationalisation for some previous action, rather than the underlying rationale from which the acquisition programme is derived.

If the acquisition strategy is to serve as the basis for a successful acquisition programme, it must meet certain requirements. In the first instance the strategy should serve to identify the role that acquisition can play in enhancing a purely organic business development approach, and establish the value-creation logic underlying the acquisition. Thereafter, it should set the acquisition parameters (i.e. the ideal characteristics of the target company) so as to guide the subsequent searching and screening activities.

With these objectives in mind, an acquisition strategy should contain at least the following elements:

1. A review of the competitive positioning and market environment of the base businesses, combined with some insight on how these will evolve.
2. An assessment of the likelihood of achieving a sustainably advantaged position for the business over some future period under various organic development options, and an analysis of the financial consequences and resource requirements of each of the leading options.
3. The identification of alternative acquisition routes which could meet these resource requirements, and a comparative evaluation of acquisitive and organic options.
4. A clear statement of the value-creation logic underpinning the acquisition, either by improving the target's performance or by identifying and exploiting synergies.
5. An analysis of the likely financial implications of acquisition, with particular focus upon future profitability, gearing and the impact upon earnings per share.
6. An initial review of the risks involved, ideally with reference to representative takeover targets.
7. A statement of the key acquisition criteria to be used in searching for and screening candidate companies, and the target timetable and project responsibilities.

The depth with which those seven considerations should be addressed will clearly depend upon the specific complexities of each individual situation. Equally, the focus and priorities of the analysis will vary from one company to the next, dependent upon whether the acquisition rationale is being driven by the need to strengthen the core business or by diversification considerations. But in all cases, the acquisition strategy must meet the requirements of identifying the value-creation logic and providing a clear guide for subsequent action.

By looking at acquisition strategy in this way, it immediately becomes obvious that, first, acquisition strategy is a derivative of business strategy (and not, as is all too often the case, the other way round); and secondly, it can only be formulated by means of a structured, analytical process. This is illustrated schematically in Figure 1.1.

Reducing the process to a series of steps in this way is clearly a simplification. It is seldom, if ever, possible to work through the creation of an acquisition strategy in as sequential a manner as the flowchart implies. Inevitably, there is a continual iteration between establishing the

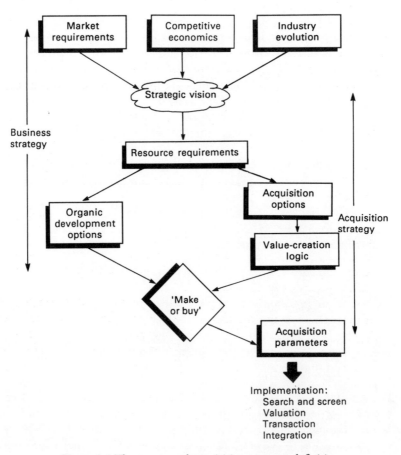

Figure 1.1 The process of acquisition strategy definition

strategic vision and exploring the practical realities of the various business development options. But the more the process can be approached with a disciplined structure, and the more clearly the strategic vision and resulting resource requirements can be identified before considering the particulars of the acquisition, the more likely it is that the acquisition strategy will prove to be robust.

Establishing the strategic vision

Acquisition is a tool of business strategy. It is only one of many competing ways by which a company can meet its strategic objectives. If these objectives are poorly specified, or fail to recognise the underlying competitive realities, it is more than likely that the subsequent acquisition strategy will not succeed.

It follows from this that the starting point to any acquisition programme is a clearly defined and articulated business strategy. Volumes have been written on the subject of formulating strategy and, as is the case with most aspects of business management, there are no simple prescriptions. There are, none the less, a set of basic principles underlying successful strategy development which may serve as some useful guidelines:

1. Business success comes from establishing, and defending, a position of competitive advantage. In general, a competitive advantage means being able to supply a range of products and services at a lower cost than competitors or, by virtue of some proprietary feature, being able consistently to achieve a price premium in the marketplace.
2. Competitive advantage is normally associated with market leadership. For some businesses, such as mainframe computers or passenger aircraft, the relevant definition of the market is global. For others, such as printing or specialist engineering, market leadership may be better defined in niche terms, either geographically or against some particular customer subset.
3. Not all industries offer the potential for a sustainable competitive advantage. In many industries, there is inherently little scope for competitive differentiation and the margins for all competitors tend to be low. For firms competing in these industries, some form of diversification may be a strategic requirement.
4. Business strategy is the identification of ways to achieve a competitive advantage and, thereafter, to sustain it. Business strategy must address the questions of where to compete, in terms of geography and customer segment, and how to compete, in terms of product and service range and positioning, technology choice and operational structure.

5. Industries evolve as a result of competitive initiatives, external market forces and technology developments. A requirement of business strategy is the identification of the pace and nature of this evolution, to ensure that advantage can be maintained as the nature of competition changes.

In practical terms, the process of business strategy development should start with an analysis of market requirements, competitive economics and the nature of industry evolution. The objective of this work is to answer some relatively straightforward questions. What does it take to compete successfully, both now and in the future? How well positioned am I? What changes must I make in order to secure the high ground?

It is the answers to these questions which can be assembled to create the strategic vision – the statement of objectives regarding where and how the firm will compete, and the logic of why this positioning represents one of competitive advantage. Armed with this vision, it is possible to identify and select from the range of alternatives for meeting these objectives; without it, there is seldom the bedrock of understanding to ensure that decisions are taken correctly and consistently.

As anyone who has ever attempted to formulate a business strategy will immediately appreciate, the preceding analysis is a deceptive over-simplification. A vast amount of information, most of which is extremely difficult to access, is required to undertake the analysis. And even if the data were available, the conceptual and analytical complexities are daunting, and considerable investments of managerial time and effort are required. There are no easy solutions to these problems, other than to recognise that the disciplines of sound strategic management will not be acquired overnight and must be built up gradually and progressively, with continual encouragement and leadership from the top. It is usually advisable to involve as broad a cross-section of management as possible in the strategy formulation process, to ensure that all internal information sources are being tapped and to develop consensus regarding the chosen direction. And it may, on occasion, be helpful to use outside consultants to assist in the process, particularly in those situations where sensitive external information is required and where the consultant, travelling incognito, may have easier access.

Articulating the strategic vision in some form of document is an important part of the process. Committing the strategic objectives, and the analysis which underpins their formulation, to paper forces a level of rigour; it also facilitates the communication, debate and consensus-building which are all critical dimensions of the strategy development process.

Establishing the strategic vision brings into focus the desired competitive positioning for the business. It also leads directly to two fundamental questions:

1. Is the vision feasible and, if so, what additional resources will be required to achieve it?
2. Even if it can be achieved, does it meet shareholder requirements?

Feasibility is often difficult to address in the abstract. Whilst some obvious tests of feasibility can be applied at this level (based, for example, upon considerations of funding availability, technology development requirements and management capability), it is generally better to leave the rigorous feasibility assessment until quite tangible development options have been identified and explored. Clarifying the additional resource requirements, on the other hand, is a process which cannot be side-stepped; correctly defined, they form the basis for all future business development activity, be it organic or acquisition-based.

The incremental resource requirements may be defined in a number of ways. They may be asset-based (such as manufacturing plant, distribution facilities or testing laboratories), technology-based (such as new products, new processes or enhanced R & D capabilities), or human resource-based (such as extended sales and marketing presence or specific new functional skills), or some combination of all the above. They may be in the same geographical markets as the existing business or in some currently unserved markets. They may, where gaining market share is a key strategic objective, be identical in nature to the existing resource base of the firm, or they may represent an extension, either vertically or horizontally, into a related business area.

The issue of acceptability of the strategic vision in terms of shareholder requirements often poses some thorny questions. Where the business unit is a subsidiary, it may be that at group level, specific performance criteria are laid down and, in these circumstances, the test of shareholder acceptability can be applied in a straightforward manner. BAT Industries, for example, imposes on all of its subsidiaries unambiguous requirements for growth, profitability and cashflow. More typically, the question of what represents adequacy as regards financial outlook is not crystal-clear; it is only by reference to broad 'rules-of-thumb', based on historic performance, competitors' performance and standards from other industries that the issue can be addressed.

To the extent that shareholders' requirements cannot be met, the question of diversification must enter the equation. This most obviously occurs in mature industries where, even for the best-positioned competitors, growth prospects and profit margins may fall short of requirements. Alternatively, the need to diversify may be driven by the recognition that the base business is hopelessly disadvantaged competitively and no realistic likelihood of improving this position can be engineered.

Business theorists have, for many years, argued against the wisdom of diversification and, indeed, there is much compelling evidence to suggest that the risks of attempting to enter new businesses tend to outweigh the likely rewards for the shareholders. This may be cold comfort to the management and employees when faced with a progressive erosion of their business and livelihoods, and the reconciliation of mutually conflicting objectives of shareholders and employees is often difficult. There is no general rule for addressing this dilemma. What can be stated with some conviction, however, is that if diversification is to be attempted, it should be in as related a business as possible and approached with an exaggerated level of caution, with all that implies for the frequency and rigour of progress monitoring.

Relating this back to the strategy framework, it may be that the original strategic vision, having failed the test of shareholder acceptability, is replaced, or augmented, by another which has more of a diversification orientation. This does not, however, diminish in any way the requirement to spell out clearly the chosen competitive positioning (in this case, for both the core business and for the diversification initiative), and the resources required to achieve this.

Creating value through acquisitions

It is only in the context of a clearly identified set of resource requirements, dictated by the business strategy, that the merits of acquisition can be explored. And even here, the appropriate base case, against which the acquisition should be evaluated, is the organic development alternative.

In essence, acquisitions pose a 'make or buy' decision, similar in concept to the decision that a manufacturer faces when confronted with the choice of investing in new plant to make a certain component, or purchasing that component from an outside supplier. This is a routine business decision, evaluated on the basis of economic, timing and risk considerations.

These same three factors apply in the case of acquisition versus organic development. It may be that the strategic vision highlights the requirement to broaden a product range, upgrade a technology base or penetrate a foreign market. Choosing the appropriate method, be it internal development or acquisition, is a question of economics, timing and risk. And it should not be forgotten that the choice is seldom unequivocal: there may well be some intermediate options involving joint venture, licensing or agency relationships.

The process of formulating the acquisition strategy involves a sequence of steps:

1. Document the major resource requirements dictated by the business strategy in as much detail as possible.
2. Use this understanding to develop an 'ideal' set of characteristics that various types of acquisition should have.
3. Examine the funding capability of the firm, in terms of both incremental debt and equity, and establish what constraints, if any, are likely to be imposed upon an acquisition programme by earnings dilution considerations.
4. Conduct some simple tests of reasonableness; within the financial constraints imposed by funding considerations, assess the likelihood, on a preliminary basis, that there are sufficient available targets to make a serious acquisition search worthwhile.
5. Examine the value-creation logic underlying the acquisition strategy to ensure that the intended benefits are real and sufficient to overcome the costs involved.
6. Compare the attractiveness of acquisition against the options of organic development or alternative forms of strategic alliance.
7. Establish the screening criteria and develop a plan, in which responsibilities and timetables are identified, for executing the acquisition search.

The process is seldom as sequential and mechanical as these seven steps imply. As a practical matter, a balance needs to be struck between two alternative approaches: developing the acquisition strategy either in abstract terms (i.e. constructing an 'ideal' acquisition candidate, and then searching for targets which most closely fit the ideal profile) or by reference to specific known companies. In this respect, a more conventional shopping analogy can be drawn. For some, a trip to a supermarket is preceded by a careful review of needs and the preparation of a shopping list; for others, a meander around the shelves is necessary to bring the needs into focus. For most of us, some combination of the two approaches works best.

In the development of an acquisition strategy, it is usually advisable to work through the process initially at a relatively conceptual level, to develop a first-cut appreciation of the potential benefits of acquisition and to set some basic screening criteria. Thereafter, some 'reference' targets should be identified, and the whole process repeated. In this way, greater depth and rigour can be added to the analysis and a more pragmatic perspective on benefits, costs and risks can be developed. And finally, when the detailed searching and screening of target candidates is underway, the underlying strategy should be frequently revisited and refined on the basis of the new information which is being obtained and the competitive insights which it is yielding.

Of all of the steps involved in formulating the acquisition strategy, as detailed above, by far the most critical (and the one most frequently overlooked) is the examination of the value-creating logic. Acquisitions are expensive. In recent years, the premium to be paid over market value for gaining control of a public company has been in the range of 30–50 per cent and, in some cases, substantially higher. This is nominally less the case for smaller, private acquisitions, but even here the transaction fees can add appreciably to the price of the acquisition. It is self-evident that value must be created by the purchase to justify these premia, and this may be accomplished by some combination of exploiting synergies of combination and improving the stand-alone performance of the acquired business.

By far the more reliable method of value-creation is the exploitation of synergies between acquirer and acquiree. This may take many forms: consolidation of staff functions and overheads, capturing scale economies in distribution, rationalisation of the combined manufacturing configuration, and superior purchasing leverage, to name but a few. The critical point is that the synergies must have a real economic foundation, they must be identifiable in advance of the transaction and they must be sufficient in magnitude to warrant paying the acquisition premium.

Most studies of acquisition performance have highlighted the fact that the more related the acquisition is to the base business, the more likely it is to succeed. This is hardly a surprising observation. If two businesses are related in terms of markets, manufacturing requirements, technology characteristics or management systems, the potential to realise genuine synergies of combination is high. Diversification through acquisition is recognised to be a highly risky proposition, partly because of the pitfalls posed by unfamiliarity, but largely because of the absence of opportunities to exploit synergy.

In general, an acquisition strategy which has been developed by considering the resource requirements dictated by the business strategy, will automatically create opportunities for synergy. But this will not always be the case. Particularly when cross-border acquisitions are being considered, genuine synergistic benefits may be scarce, despite a clear long-term strategic fit. It may be that the competitive strategic considerations should predominate and the acquisition premium should be viewed as an unrecoupable, but none the less acceptable, penalty . . . but, in these situations, it is strongly advisable to re-examine non-acquisitive options for developing the business. There may well be less expensive ways to put in place the necessary resources.

Improving the stand-alone performance of the acquired business can seldom be relied upon as a basis for value-creation. Of course, there are poorly managed businesses, the performance of which can be upgraded by the injection of better management and some tight financial controls. And there are companies, such as BTR, which have demonstrable skills in this regard. But 'turnaround' expertise is highly specialised, and those acquirers who possess it have built up their skills over many years. As a general rule, the performance of a business is more directly related to its structural competitive positioning than to the capabilities of its management. Furthermore, most managements have a tendency to overestimate their own competence, and correspondingly, to underestimate that of a potential acquisition target. With these observations in mind, a safe operating rule is to be extremely wary of 'turnarounds' when considering acquisition.

It is not uncommon for companies to consider acquisition for reasons which are only indirectly linked to competitive strategic requirements; most typically, these are:

1. To improve short-term earnings per share, by acquisition of a company with a lower earnings multiple.
2. To restructure the balance sheet, using an acquisition programme as a convenient vehicle for attracting further equity and/or altering the shareholder profile.
3. To upgrade existing management.
4. To improve visibility with an investment community, often in another country.

For many companies, these are genuine needs and an acquisition programme may well assist in meeting them. But these are seldom, if ever, adequate bases for creating value. A takeover which is predicated solely upon some combination of these objectives is unlikely to merit the acquisition premium. These factors should be relegated to a secondary level in establishing the attractiveness of an acquisition strategy: desirable, perhaps, but not fundamental.

In summary, acquisition is only one of many tools of corporate development, and should always be evaluated against organic alternatives. There are no firm rules for choosing between acquisition and internal development – it depends upon whichever method offers the superior prospect of meeting the strategic objectives at the lowest cost and with the minimum risk. However, for guideline purposes, acquisition tends to be most appropriate when:

1. Timing considerations are paramount, and there is a competitive requirement to fill the resource gap quickly.

2. Geographical diversification is the objective, and where the structure of the foreign business to be added closely mirrors that of the existing domestic activity.
3. Major technology additions are required and, for competitive reasons, licensing options are not available.
4. The strategy calls for vertical or horizontal integration, where significant potential synergies of combination may be present.

Setting screening criteria

The principal output of the acquisition strategy formulation process is a set of parameters to guide the subsequent searching and screening activity. It follows from the discussion of value-creation that some of these parameters are critical, while others, although possibly desirable, are of a more peripheral nature. To ensure that appropriate weighting is being given to the various screening criteria, it is usually sensible to assemble them in some form of rank order:

1. *Primary criteria: strategic contribution*
   (a) Size, nature of business, location,
   (b) Competitive positioning and prospects,
   (c) Specific resource requirements (such as technology base, manufacturing assets, sales force configuration, head office structure).
2. *Secondary criteria: financial acceptability*
   (a) Profitability and cashflow requirements,
   (b) Balance sheet requirements,
   (c) P/E ratio,
   (d) Shareholder profile,
   (e) Stockmarket listing requirements.
3. *Tertiary criteria: other considerations*
   (a) Management capabilities,
   (b) City profile,
   (c) Financial engineering potential (such as sale/leaseback opportunities, or unrealised assets).

In the first instance, these criteria should form the basis of the search activity, to identify a shortlist of targets which appear to fit the required profile. Thereafter, the same criteria can be used to establish the framework for analysing the shortlisted companies, and discriminating across them.

The process of acquisition strategy definition does not stop with the establishment of screening criteria. A number of important practical dimensions to the acquisition strategy can only be addressed in the context of evaluating specific targets, and it is of vital importance that these issues are kept in the forefront as the programme unfolds:

1. Can a hostile bid be entertained? Is management willing to subject themselves to the intense public scrutiny that accompanies a hostile approach? What are the risks and costs of failure?
2. How realistic are the synergy opportunities for each target? Over what time-frame are they realisable, and with what management implications?
3. From a cultural and systems perspective, how well do the two companies fit? What is the proposed organisational model post-acquisition? How dependent is success upon the continued commitment of the target's management and what needs to be done to ensure this?
4. What will be the impact of acquisition on the balance sheet and earnings? What constraints regarding funding does this impose? What are the timing implications for the transaction?

The further the screening process progresses, the more the issues become tactical, addressing the specifics of the transaction. And the more management becomes embroiled in the tactics and day-to-day negotiations, the easier it is to lose sight of the underlying strategic requirements. A thorough and well-documented acquisition strategy serves as a central foundation for the subsequent implementation process, and minimises the risk that management will either enter into an inappropriate transaction or accede to an unrealistic price.

Practical considerations in defining acquisition strategies

There are no easy prescriptions for developing effective acquisition strategies. The diversity of possible acquisition objectives, and the range of transactions which result, argue against the use of simple formulae. In common with most management activities, there is no substitute for experience; successful acquirers have learned, by trial and error, how to avoid the pitfalls and construct acquisition strategies which consistently create value.

For the less experienced purchaser, however, the following guidelines may help to improve the odds of succeeding:

1. Ensure that the acquisition strategy is derived from a clear understanding of the competitive requirements of the base business, both now and in the future. Always evaluate acquisitions against other options for achieving a position of competitive advantage, be they purely organic or some form of strategic alliance.
2. Avoid acquisitions where the underlying rationale is heavily depend-

ent upon short-term financial objectives (such as improving earnings per share or providing the opportunity to restructure the balance sheet). Also, avoid 'turnarounds' or situations where the acquisition is only justifiable on the assumption of major improvements in the target's performance.

3. Structure the strategy formulation process carefully, with a thoughtful delineation of the task sequence, responsibilities and timetable. 'Brainstorming' sessions may be a helpful adjunct to the process, but they should support, not replace, the basic analytical sequence.

4. Document the acquisition strategy and its underlying logic. Apart from the rigour that this imposes, such a strategy document is an invaluable aid to internal debate and consensus-building.

5. Be sure that the synergies identified are real and quantifiable. Vague concepts of 'fit' are unreliable. Most experienced purchasers recognise that transferring resources across companies and/or eliminating duplicated costs is a difficult and time-consuming process.

6. Involve a broad cross-section of management as early as possible. At the end of the day, all levels of management will be responsible for making the acquisition work; the broader the base of internal commitment to the strategy, the more likely it is to succeed.

7. Seek outside advice from business acquaintances and professional advisers. They can assist in identifying inconsistencies in the strategy, finding appropriate target companies, and recognising the practicalities of the transaction which may impose constraints on the search.

8. Develop an abstract perspective on why, and in what form, an acquisition is desirable, before embarking upon a search. As part of this process, it may be helpful to use certain potential acquisition candidates as reference points to test the quality of the thinking. But reserve the detailed searching until the key screening criteria have been identified and agreed.

9. Develop an understanding of funding practicalities and, in the case of private companies, ownership requirements early in the process, so that these can be incorporated in the screening criteria. However, avoid detailed funding issues, such as the appropriate weighting and structure of debt and equity financing, until specific transactions have been identified.

10. Don't wait to be sold a company. There is clear evidence that most poor acquisitions are seller-initiated. In these situations the balance between desirability and availability is disturbed, and it is easy for judgement to become clouded. Maintaining an opportunistic outlook is appropriate, but it should not be a central feature of an acquisition strategy.

11. Be wary of over-excitement and over-optimism. The adrenalin boost created by the prospect of making an acquisition can easily lead to poor decision-making.

Chapter 2

Finding suitable businesses

MICHAEL J. D. STALLIBRASS

Executive Director, Shearson Lehman Hutton International, Inc.

Introduction

The way in which a company embarks upon the process of identifying suitable businesses for acquisition depends greatly on the specific characteristics of the acquirer company. Thus, the extent to which the acquirer is able or prepared to commit management time to the search process, the size of the business being sought, the nature of the acquisition, whether add-on or diversification, and the appetite for acquisitions, will all, to a greater or lesser extent, influence the route adopted. Certain fundamental procedures should, however, be instigated and these can best be described under the general heading of preparing oneself for the acquisition process.

In Chapter 1, the method in which a company should draw up its acquisition strategy was discussed. This exercise in itself will have taken the acquirer some way down the road towards creating the correct infrastructure and corporate frame of mind to embark upon the search for suitable acquisitions. It is the steps that are taken after that somewhat introspective stage that are important in determining the number and quality of acquisition opportunities presented for consideration.

It must be understood at the outset that the whole acquisition process, from development of strategy, through identification of suitable candidates, analysis, negotiation and consummation of the transaction, is likely to require considerable management time. For this process to be managed in a concerted and structured fashion, the company should designate a senior member of management to be responsible for implementing the acquisition strategy. While this function may not be the sole responsibility of the individual concerned it should not be seen as an occasional diversion to be fitted in between other, more pressing, matters. Timing, and the ability to react in a timely fashion to situations as they arise, are key elements in the company being able to find and acquire suitable businesses.

The position of the acquisitions function within the organisation will depend upon the composition and structure of the company's management team. Some companies set up a separate acquisitions unit, which should in any event be relatively narrowly staffed; others combine the role with the finance or planning departments. Whichever method is chosen, the individual or unit concerned must have direct access to, and the active support of, the chief executive (or similarly senior Board member). Without this support the conviction that is required on the part of the company if it is to pursue acquisitions to a satisfactory conclusion is undermined.

Irrespective of the size of the acquisitions team, it is essential to the whole search process that all acquisitions opportunities are first passed to the team. This not only avoids duplication of effort, but also enables the company to take a focused view on its strategy and make comparative judgements on opportunities that arise.

Sources of acquisition opportunities

It should be the basic tenet of any acquisitions manager that no one person or organisation can be counted upon to be aware of all suitable acquisitions prospects. Thus, the search should encompass ideas generated from three different sources:

1. the individuals responsible for the business units which make up the organisation,
2. the acquisitions unit itself, and
3. the ideas that may be brought by third parties involved in the mergers and acquisitions field.

Ideas generated from within the organisation

Business unit managers are involved in developing their individual business strategies, which are then distilled into the strategy for the group as a whole. Accordingly, they are aware, at least in part, of the acquisition aspirations of the group. Once this group-wide strategy has been developed, agreed by the Board and formalised in writing, business managers should be informed of its contents and encouraged to put forward ideas that satisfy the acquisition criteria. These managers see, at first hand, not only the strengths and weaknesses of their own businesses but also those of the organisations with which they come into contact on a day-to-day basis. Such a network is invaluable in identifying potential acquisition candidates, picking up industry gossip on companies that may be, or are likely to be, for sale, and ultimately in assisting in the analysis of companies once they have been deemed specific acquisition targets.

While all parts of the organisation have a role to play in seeking out acquisitions, the front-line troops must be the sales force. Their everyday contact with customers informs them at an early stage which businesses may be up for sale.

A business may be divested for a variety of reasons, for example, the existing shareholders may have become too old to run the business effectively and there may be no obvious succession; or the shareholders may wish to cash in and spend their money on other pursuits, for example. Regular contact between the sales force and customers is an early warning system which should be used to maximum advantage.

The sales force will also pick up information about competitors – their strengths and weaknesses, the possibility that they will be vacating certain parts of the business, etc. They may also hear, for example, that a competitor has developed a new product line. Perhaps this product line is extremely interesting to your company, and indeed, that your company has a greater capability of developing and bringing that particular product range to market.

Most good sales teams develop their business by long-term, friendly relationships with key customers. For this reason, it may well be that customers first speak to them rather than making a direct approach to management if they wish to divest their company. This longstanding relationship offers not only the advantage of letting your company know first, but also the possibility of making a friendly approach and possibly a speedy deal.

The sales force, however, is not the only part of the business which can assist in acquisitions. Members of the research department in the normal course of their business may come across new ideas in parallel companies which, taken together with existing ideas in your company, lead to a powerful combination. Alternatively, the research department might recognise the need to have a good distribution system for a new piece of technology or a new product. This could lead them to identify potential customers who could be taken over as a route to a distribution system.

Equally, other parts of the organisation – engineering, public relations, etc. – continually come into contact with situations where they are able, if they have their eyes and ears open, to come up with good ideas.

Provided that they are encouraged to put forward ideas and, as importantly, such ideas are seen to be considered seriously, these sources should provide a steady stream of promising opportunities. However, business managers will tend to uncover only add-on or fill-in acquisitions that are generally smaller than the business of which they would form a part. It is important that all parts of the business are encouraged to put forward their ideas. On the other hand, people outside the main stream of acquisitions activity must avoid the temptation actively to begin negotiations. A clear definition of responsibilities between the monitoring role, and the initiation, negotiation and purchase role must be established within the organisation.

In order to ensure that ideas are properly vetted and controlled, all internally generated ideas should always be referred back to the central acquisitions function. Their brief is not only to assess and sift these ideas but also to control a wider brief in identifying those companies which fulfil the acquisition criteria set down in the company strategy.

In the context of strategy, there is one final comment about internally generated ideas. The definition of the characteristics of a desirable acquisition are best spelled out by the people in the business. Thus the sales force or engineering or research functions may not be able to identify particular companies but they should be able to give a broad specification of the key characteristics. For example, if the desired acquisition is to provide or enhance distribution activity, the marketing force can specify the size, technical qualifications, geographical diversity and other similar characteristics. On the basis of this information the acquisitions function can form a coherent picture of the ideal candidate company.

Externally generated ideas and the use of financial intermediaries

In any attempt to tap into sources of ideas generated by third parties, the corporate acquirer is faced with a plethora of what are loosely defined as mergers and acquisitions intermediaries. The diversity of such intermediaries can be confusing to the newly appointed acquisitions manager, extending, as it does, from merchant and investment banks through accountants and consultants to business brokers, finders and other less well-defined intermediaries. The decision as to which of these experts to employ and, indeed, how many of them to contact depends to a great extent on the characteristics of the acquisitions being sought and particularly their size.

In the first instance, the corporate acquirer can adopt a relatively passive role simply by letting it be known generally that the company is acquisitive. Accordingly, to encourage intermediaries to put forward acquisition candidates, the company should take the opportunity of spelling out its intentions in published information, such as its annual report and accounts, and in discussions with the financial press, bankers, stockbrokers, analysts and employees. The successful conclusion of one or more acquisitions will make the point most forcefully. In adopting this approach, however, the corporate acquirer must be fully committed to making acquisitions, to avoid overreaching the company by building expectations too high. The company and its management may lose credibility if its by then well-documented acquisition strategy does not bear fruit within a reasonable period of time.

Some companies may feel that with the increased competition between investment banks, merchant banks and other external advisers to generate fees, such intermediaries need little encouragement to bring them acquisition opportunities. This misses the point, for while a company will want it to be known that it is acquisitive, its main task is to elicit ideas which conform as closely as possible to its acquisition criteria and to hear of companies which can, in fact, be acquired.

The passive approach described above should help put the company in touch with the flow of mergers and acquisitions opportunities in the market, but in most circumstances the would-be acquirer will want to be more pro-active in its approach.

Companies normally discuss their acquisition criteria with their financial advisers; indeed, the criteria may have been developed in consultation with them. However, to limit these discussions to only two or three specialists is to reduce substantially the possibilities of finding a suitable target. It would not be unusual, or indeed unprofessional, to circulate a summary of the company's criteria to a fairly wide range of financial intermediaries. This summary should be as specific and informative as possible and should generally include:

1. a description of the nature of the business being sought,
2. its size in revenue or profit terms,
3. its preferred location,
4. the anticipated method of purchase, and
5. the requirement or otherwise for management continuity.

It cannot be stressed too strongly that a loose description such as 'an engineering business with revenues of up to £200 million within the EEC' will almost certainly elicit no response from intermediaries and, indeed, may, from its imprecision, wrongly suggest that the company is not serious in its intent.

As the acquisition search progresses, so companies will find some intermediaries much more helpful than others in identifying suitable opportunities. This process will inevitably lead to a reduction in the number of M & A specialists with whom an active dialogue is maintained. However, the company should not discourage any intermediaries from bringing ideas to them, unless, of course, they are thought to be acting unprofessionally or simply fishing for information.

As the company develops its relationships with those intermediaries who have proved their capability, or interest, in assisting in the acquisition search so it should take time to discuss with them, in more detail, the way in which its strategy has been drawn up and the manner in which it is being developed in the continuation of the search for, or the completion of, transactions. This will enable the intermediary to keep up-to-date with the company's acquisition criteria and improve understanding of the business and culture of the acquirer. This should ultimately lead to the recommendation of only those situations which are clearly within or closely allied to the criteria.

Equally important in developing relationships is the responsiveness of the corporate acquirer to acquisition ideas. A speedy response to situations that are of no interest, with, where appropriate, a short explanation why, should not be difficult. The acquisition manager should not be embarrassed to turn down ideas which are clearly not appropriate. The intelligent intermediary will not be discouraged if cogent reasons are given, but will rather see it as a learning process which should help in presenting more appropriate opportunities in the future. If a quick response is not possible, or indeed if the situation is of interest, then, once again, the intermediary should be kept informed of the progress being made by the company.

By adopting such an approach, the corporate acquirer will be seen as a company to be called early on in the development of any potential acquisition and will be considered a serious 'player' by originators of transactions. Accordingly, they will tend to be shown a greater number of viable opportunities than those companies whose decision-making process is slow or lacking in critique.

When making contact with financial intermediaries it is important to understand the distinction between the different types of professionals and the contribution they are able, or may expect, to make towards the successful conclusion of a transaction. It is equally important to match the skills of the particular individual to your requirements and to establish, in advance, the exact role you wish the intermediary to play in the development and execution of your acquisition search.

Broadly speaking, intermediaries can be divided into three categories (though one should beware of differences in their and your terminology) each providing a different level of service.

The business broker

The business broker is usually an individual who acts as a matchmaker between buyers and sellers in his particular business community. (In the USA the same function is called a 'finder'.) The business broker relies primarily on personal contacts, with whom the subjects of businesses that may be for sale or acquirers looking for acquisition opportunities are raised. Accordingly, the broker spends little time analysing the business of the seller or the needs of the buyer. It is in the nature of the way in which such individuals carry out their search that they let the marketplace know of both the buyers' and sellers' intentions. Accordingly, it would be inadvisable to engage a business broker if confidentiality is paramount.

The capabilities of finders vary enormously. Before entering into any arrangements it is as well to establish their particular expertise and track record, including, if appropriate, requesting references from previous clients.

Generally a business broker will simply introduce the acquirer to parties with whom a transaction may be arranged. The broker will not expect to participate in negotiations, nor to advise on valuation or other related matters. The business broker is normally involved in transactions of less than $5 million and remunerated on a success-only basis.

M & A consultants

M & A consultants offer a broader range of services than the business broker and are usually engaged in small to medium-sized transactions in the $5–50 million range. In the USA, where they are sometimes confusingly referred to as 'business brokers', they are normally regional firms with contacts throughout their particular geographic area. They should have established a reputation, built up over a number of years, for undertaking transactions involving companies in their locale. Some M & A consultants specialise in identifying opportunities in a specific industry sector, the knowledge of which has been built up from an individual's direct business experience in that field. In the UK and Europe, their geographic focus tends to be national, although, as in the USA, they specialise in transactions which are considered to be too small to attract the attention of the merchant or investment banks.

In contrast to the business broker, who simply tries to match buyers and sellers, and is not necessarily a specialist in mergers and acquisitions, M & A consultants are usually established players in the M & A market. As such, they will take time to understand the client's business and its acquisition criteria and should be able to carry out detailed searches for acquisition targets, which may include the preparation of market research studies and detailed valuation reports. The M & A consultant should also be capable of conducting negotiations on the client's behalf. It is important to establish in advance how far the M & A consultant will be expected to go in an acquisition search for the client and whether the consultant will be expected to advise on valuation or to participate in negotiations. If the engagement does include a search mandate, a retainer fee is likely to be charged for that part of the exercise, as well as a success fee.

The financial adviser

This broad term includes merchant banks, investment banks and the specialist M & A departments of some large accounting firms, stockbrokers and commercial banks.

With their constant involvement in merger and acquisition transactions of all types and in all industries, firms falling within this category are well placed to identify suitable acquisition candidates. In addition, the financial adviser is able to provide advice on the valuation, negotiation and financing of the transaction and will expect to be involved from the beginning of the acquisition programme through to closure.

Fees

In general terms, the fee payable to an intermediary will depend on the size of the transaction and the nature and extent of the services provided. Accordingly, the structure of the fee agreement and the amount of the fee will vary from assignment to assignment and intermediary to intermediary. It is essential, therefore, that both the acquirer and the intermediary have an understanding, which should be set out in writing, of the fee obligation prior to embarking upon the exercise. The agreement should set out clearly how the fees are to be calculated, when the fees are to be paid, and the services that are to be provided by the intermediary in terms of assistance in valuation, negotiations, documentation and related matters. Such detailed agreements avoid the possibility of unpleasant misunderstandings at the conclusion of the acquisition.

Fees may be agreed under two distinct headings:

1. a retainer, which is normally paid at the time at which the adviser is retained, and
2. a success fee which is paid immediately after the successful consummation of a transaction.

Retainer fees, which can usually be offset against any success fee, are unpopular in some circles. However, when a would-be acquirer engages an intermediary to undertake a search of a specific industry sector or to embark upon negotiations which may be protracted, the request for payment of a modest fee is not unreasonable. In essence, this is no more than a recognition of the fact that the intermediary will commit time and expertise to the undertaking.

There are no hard-and-fast rules as to the amount that should be paid for retainer or success fees. Generally speaking, the former should loosely reflect the time that it is anticipated will be spent by the intermediary in completing that part of the total service, whereas the latter will normally be calculated on the basis of a percentage of the transaction size.

In the past, the so-called 'Lehman scale' was most often quoted as the basis for calculating success fees on small transactions. Under this formula, 5 per cent was paid on the first $1 million of the transaction, 4 per cent on the next $1 million, 3 per cent on the next $1 million, 2 per cent on the next $1 million and 1 per cent on any amount in excess of $4 million. More recently the fees quoted on these smaller transactions have increased, and the Lehman scale is seldom used as the basis for remuneration, having been superseded by either higher percentages at the lower end of the scale or the same percentages being applied to larger tranches of the transaction price.

For medium-sized and larger transactions, the success fee is most often expressed as a fixed percentage of the transaction value. Acquirers may now expect to pay 0.5 per cent for sizeable transactions (i.e. in excess of some $250 million) and around 1.5 per cent for transactions of some $50 million. Needless to say, there are many variations. Alternative ways of structuring the success fee may include some form of incentive for the intermediary to extract the best deal for his client. When the client is the buyer, this may be expressed in terms of an upwards ratchet on the percentage, the lower the price paid by the acquirer (the converse being the case when the client is the seller). While sophisticated fee structures may sound appealing, one should not get too carried away with the negotiation of a complicated fee agreement; better to save such negotiating flair for the acquisition in hand and rely upon the professional integrity of the intermediary to assist in obtaining the best transaction.

However the fee agreement is proposed, the acquirer should remember that the fee is often negotiable, but only at the outset. It must be remembered though that a thorough and professional job is seldom undertaken for a cut-price fee.

Managing the search process

It was suggested earlier that a company embarking upon a serious acquisition programme should designate a suitably senior member of management to oversee the acquisition process. This individual must decide at the start how to staff and manage this operation.

Two decisions will have to be made immediately. First, the company will need to decide whether it intends to adopt an active or passive approach in its search for suitable acquisitions. Secondly, a decision will have to be taken as to the extent to which the company itself undertakes the work involved in identifying acquisition candidates or whether this is given to third parties. Much of the work involved can be carried out by intermediaries and the business broker, the M & A consultant and the financial adviser should all have the necessary skills. In some instances, the search may form part of a general review of the business carried out by a management consultant or take the form of an in-depth study by them of an industry sector of interest to the acquirer. An exercise of this nature, carried out by a third party is, however, likely to be costly and the committed acquirer may, therefore, prefer to undertake at least the initial screening of acquisition candidates itself. Indeed, it may be argued that the knowledge gained at first hand from being involved in an active search, is, in general, a prerequisite to the success of the corporate acquirer's endeavours. Not all companies have personnel available to spend the whole of their time engaged in an active search for acquisition candidates, but it will rapidly become apparent that the passive approach produces potential acquisitions of wide-ranging quality that may already have been hawked around or which are subject to an auction process. This does not mean that the acquirer should necessarily reject the latter, provided it is understood that in such an environment the competitive element of the auction will generally lead to a higher price being paid and a limit being put on the time available to analyse and assess the merits of the target.

The active approach, while expensive in management time, undoubtedly leads to a better understanding of the candidates. This will, in turn, assist in a better definition of the acquisition criteria and whether, in fact, it appears they can be satisfied; an appreciation of the competitive position of the companies within the chosen market; and a more fundamental understanding of what the acquirer will be faced with when the acquisition is made.

At the same time as the various phases of the active search process are unfolding, the company should take steps to encourage intermediaries to bring ideas to them (the passive strategy). In general, such situations will involve companies that are definitely for sale or seriously contemplating such a step, although this will not always be the case. An attentive intermediary may well introduce the acquirer to situations where a sale may be induced, for example where there is a dissatisfied significant shareholder or a boardroom disagreement. Such an opportunity may enable the acquirer to make a pre-emptive move and secure a business before its potential sale becomes widely known. Clearly, in the light of what has been said about the auction process, such an opportunity may be very attractive. It is at this stage that the well-prepared acquirer will reap the rewards of his diligence. However, before aggressively following up such leads, the acquisitions manager should endeavour to discover the reality of this 'scoop' and determine that the lead represents more than just an exercise in flying kites.

As the search proceeds and ideas are brought in by intermediaries, the corporate acquirer will be building up a substantial amount of information, a major portion of which will not be of immediate consequence. This intelligence should not be discarded but should form a database that can be used in the future to analyse and possibly revisit potential acquisition candidates. The proper management of this database is an essential factor in increasing the likelihood of the company being able to react swiftly to acquisition opportunities.

Most ideas presented by intermediaries should be included in the database with details of the date of the contact, the intermediary's name and relationship to the business, and the basic information on the company, including if possible an estimate of the price. It is surprising how many situations take time to come to fruition and what may prove to be an unworkable acquisition today can often become a serious proposition in the future. This is particularly true of what might be called the acquirer's 'wish-list', which is made up of companies that are identified as satisfying the acquisition criteria but which, for one reason or another, cannot be immediately acquired. Time, changes in the target's circumstances and the growth through acquisition, or otherwise, of the potential acquirer may enable those 'wish-list' companies to be more actively pursued in the future.

To complete the picture, the M & A function will need to keep abreast of situations that develop in the public arena. Such information can be gleaned from the financial press, M & A publications and specialist trade magazines. In this way the acquisition manager should be aware of acquisitions taking place in the business segments of interest, rumours of businesses 'in play' and the dynamics of agglomeration or fragmentation within the sector.

Cross-border acquisitions

While the steps outlined above are as applicable to the search for international transactions as they are for domestic transactions, it is worthwhile considering some of the peculiarities that come with an international acquisitions programme. When drawing up the criteria for international acquisitions, you should be aware that many of the assumptions usually taken for granted in making a domestic acquisition may be completely inapplicable in the context of an overseas purchase. These differences in approach are equally applicable in the context of the search for acquisitions.

In searching the international arena, the acquirer will be faced with a relatively or completely new environment in a country with a different culture and with people where attitudes, motivations and behaviour may be quite different from those with which it is familiar. This will be most evident in the problems that may be encountered in maintaining proper communications with intermediaries, or even one's own management, in the country concerned.

To the extent that overseas intermediaries are engaged to assist in the search for acquisition candidates, considerably more time should be spent in explaining the acquisition criteria and the role the intermediary is expected to play in taking the matter forward. In addition, the corporate acquirer should not make the mistake of assuming that while its business and name are well known in its country of incorporation this will not necessarily be the case in the country in which the acquisition is to be made.

It is essential that a member of the M & A unit should visit the target country frequently not only to understand the environment better but also to ensure that the acquisition search is foremost in the mind of any intermediaries that have been engaged, or are anticipated to assist, in finding suitable businesses. Coordination and communication will be greatly enhanced by assigning a company executive to be present in the country to oversee the effort.

Conclusion

If the aspiring corporate acquirer has followed the steps set out above, the company should be in a position to act swiftly and decisively on opportunities that arise. Much is made of what are termed 'opportunistic transactions'; the acquisitions manager should not be lured into thinking that this is an answer to his problems. Opportunistic transactions, if they are to be seen as successful with hindsight, are generally not opportunistic but rather a swift response to situations that have arisen and which fulfil the criteria of a strategy that has been carefully prepared and tested on many occasions.

Over a period of time, potential targets will be presented which will be analysed against the company's acquisition criteria. While an absolute and rigid adherence to the template drawn up for the perfect acquisition candidate is not practical, the corporate acquirer would do well to guard against the greater excesses sometimes practised in the name of 'business judgement' or 'special situations'. These are often no more than synonyms for frustration or boredom. However, it is imperative that, as the search proceeds and the company evolves either by acquisition or organic growth, the criteria are reviewed regularly and either confirmed or adjusted.

The role of the intermediary will prove to be important not only in the identification of targets and the execution of transactions but also as a sounding board for ideas generated internally and for confirmation of market rumours. The acquirer will work best with an intermediary with whom there is an established business and personal rapport. Time should be taken to cultivate this, for it will undoubtedly be tested in the moments of stress which frequently accompany the acquisition exercise.

As a final point, it must be appreciated that by the time the acquirer has gone through the whole process from search to analysis to actual acquisition, the success rate is low. This should not be seen as a reason for abandoning the chase. The whole acquisition exercise is something of an iterative process and something of a scientific or bureaucratic process. It is certainly a process that requires patience and cannot be founded on impulse.

Chapter 3

Methods of financial valuation

JOHN ALLDAY
Ernst & Whinney

Introduction

In the acquisition of a target company or a business its valuation is crucial to success, for it serves as the basis for the agreement between buyer and seller and determines the amount of debt and equity finance needed. Ultimately, the monetary value of anything is what somebody is prepared to pay for it. This may not sound very scientific, so is there any point in looking at methods of valuation? The short answer is yes, because most company purchases are made for commercial reasons and to enter into negotiations for the purchase of a company without a guide to its worth to the purchaser is certainly less than advisable and probably downright foolish. Valuation is an essential step in the process of buying or selling a company and at the very least it should be used to determine the maximum price the purchaser ought to pay.

A valuation is only as good as the information upon which it is based. It is therefore important to make a thorough investigation and detailed research into all aspects of the company's business.

There are a number of valuation techniques and the most appropriate can only be judged when the company's activities have been ascertained. For example, a property investment company is normally valued on a different basis from that applicable to a property dealing company. Sometimes a company might have both property dealing and property investment activities and in these circumstances it would be necessary to consider each activity separately. Moreover it is often necessary to apply more than one valuation technique in determining the actual value of a company.

The two most common approaches to valuation are by reference to earnings and assets but there are other methods which, generally speaking, can be related to an earnings basis – for example, those based on super-profits, discounted cashflow and specific trade practices.

The earnings basis of valuation

This is the most common method of valuation because it is usually the appropriate basis of valuation for the majority of trading companies, whose principal objective is to obtain a return by way of profits as opposed to primarily by way of capital appreciation. Such companies must be distinguished from those whose return is primarily derived from capital gains.

Put simply, the value on an earnings basis is arrived at by estimating maintainable profits and applying a suitable capitalisation factor. The valuer's skill lies in being able to judge future profitability and to select an appropriate profit multiple.

Maintainable profits

Probably the most common mistake when calculating maintainable profits is to forget that the value of a company reflects its future returns, whether by way of profits or capital realisations. Historic performance may be useful but it is only relevant in so far as it helps to ascertain future prospects. The valuation must be based on the company's future prospects; the past should only be used as a guide to the likely future return.

Nevertheless it is usual, and can be very useful, to consider historic trading results. There is no set period which should be examined, but in practice the last 3–5 years are normally sufficient. It is important that historic results are examined to make sure they are a true reflection of the business as it exists at the valuation date. Some points to watch for are:

1. The purchase or sale of subsidiaries or businesses, in which case the results for the review period should be adjusted to compare like with like.
2. Any change of accounting policies during the period under review.
3. Any non-commercial arrangements. Common examples are directors' loan accounts, inter-company loans other than on normal commercial terms and excessive directors' remuneration.
4. Exceptional or extraordinary items if they are unlikely to be repeated. But such items can often provide clues to an under- or overvaluation of assets, for instance a surplus on the sale of land can indicate property in the balance-sheet at a substantial undervaluation or a land bank held within the business.

The next step is to see if the adjusted historic profits indicate any pattern or tradecycle. If there is a consistent trend, either upwards or downwards, then it is inappropriate for valuation purposes to estimate maintainable earnings by taking an average, whether weighted or not.

In these circumstances the value of the business should be determined by reference to projected profits, or in their absence the latest year's earnings. However if the historic trading results show the business to be cyclical or if the trading performance fluctuates, some form of averaging will be appropriate.

The figures below illustrate some interesting possibilities:

Year ended 31 December	1983	1984	1985	1986	1987
	£000	£000	£000	£000	£000
Turnover	1,000	2,000	1,500	4,000	4,000
Profits	250	600	400	1,200	1,500

The reason for the decline in turnover and profits in 1985 is all-important. If it can be reasonably inferred that this was a one-off occurrence, the valuer might assume an upward trend, perhaps adopting 1987's profits or making a projection above the 1987 level.

However, let us assume 1985 cannot be treated as exceptional and that the figures highlight another problem. If the valuer were to look at the last three years only he would see an upward trend in profits, but if he were to look at five years he would see an inconsistent trend. The valuer looking at three years might reasonably adopt 1987's profit of £1.5 million or a higher projection as being maintainable while the valuer reviewing five years might adopt the simple average of £790,000 for those years. This illustrates the pitfalls of using historic trading results without detailed enquiry and understanding. Moreover it illustrates the dangers of placing emphasis on results which, because of their age and the growth of the company, are less likely to represent the company's present trading potential. The further back in time the valuer looks, the greater the risk that the earlier results will have little or no relevance to the value. Inflation may be an important factor to consider when analysing profit trends.

The illustrated figures give rise to another point. In 1987 turnover was static but profits increased compared to the year before. The valuer, if the facts are not already known, must ascertain the cause to decide what effect this will have on maintainable profits. Variations in turnover and gross profit margins are only relevant in so far as they bring to the valuer's attention possible factors which might influence the future level of maintainable profits.

Any conclusion reached following a review of historic profits must be tested against other available information. For instance, to take an extreme example, the review might indicate five years of decline, but a reorganisation, change of management, new products or improved outlook for the industry might all mean that historic information is less than a reliable guide to future earnings.

The valuer must now look into the future without the assistance of a crystal ball. A properly prepared forecast will be the most appropriate guide to earnings in the foreseeable future, but any forecast must be thoroughly examined to ensure that the underlying assumptions are reasonable and consistent with one's understanding of the business.

It is customary to compare earlier forecasts to actual results to test the historic reliability of the forecasts. In fairness, a forecast should not be dismissed because previous forecasts have proved unreliable. The reason for earlier discrepancies must be examined and the validity of the assumptions then made must be critically tested.

The current forecast should be reviewed in the light of all information available to the valuer, including the outlook for the industry, product or service. Does the company have sufficient liquid funds to maintain the level of profits envisaged? What about economies or diseconomies of scale in, for example, a takeover situation?

It will be reassuring if the forecast – suitably adjusted in the light of the valuer's examination – matches up with the estimation of future profits derived from historic information. If not, the valuer might adopt the forecast, assuming it is still considered the most appropriate estimate of maintainable profits, but apply a slightly different multiple to allow for the historic track record. By way of example a company with a strong growth record but whose current forecast is the same as a company with a poor track record might reasonably command a higher value. If nothing else, an impressive track record must offer some comfort at the end of the day.

Capitalisation factor

A suitable multiple must now be applied to maintainable profits. This will be either a pre-tax or post-tax multiple. The latter is usually described as a price–earnings ratio and is associated more with the value of minority holdings of shares in companies. On the sale of a company as a whole the pre-tax profit multiple is more commonly used. However, it does not matter which is used so long as there is no confusion.

The other area of possible ambiguity is whether the multiple is applied to historic or future earnings. Multiples applied to future earnings are usually described as prospective. Where a company is forecasting growth the prospective multiple will naturally be lower than the historic multiple. This is also important to bear in mind when extrapolating multiples from comparable transactions. It is incorrect to apply an historic multiple to future profits, or vice versa.

It is sometimes suggested that a pre-tax profit multiplier is preferable because it avoids the question of what Corporation Tax rate to apply to the maintainable pre-tax profits. This is illogical. How can the value of a company vary depending on the valuation approach adopted? If a pre-tax profit multiple is used this must take into account the expected taxation charge. Let us take as an example two identical companies save that company A expects to pay Corporation Tax in full at 35 per cent while company B expects to pay no Corporation Tax in the foreseeable future. Company B must have a higher value as the purchaser will obtain a greater return on his investment. This is not to say that a price–earnings ratio based on after-tax earnings is preferred for valuation purposes, merely that a pre-tax profit multiple cannot ignore taxation consequences. Thus the pre-tax multiple used to value company B, which is not expected to pay Corporation Tax, must be higher than one used to value company A which is subject to tax at the standard rate.

How then do we calculate the pre-tax profit multiple or price–earnings ratio? First, the valuer looks at actual purchases of comparable companies. These may be takeovers or mergers of companies listed on the Stock Exchange or acquisitions of unquoted companies. If there is an absence or shortage of comparable transactions, the prices of shares in companies traded on the Stock Exchange, but which are not the subject of a takeover or merger, are often used as a guide. These prices normally represent the sale of very small minority holdings. Accordingly when valuing the entire business a higher value would be appropriate. This is evidenced by the fact that on a takeover or merger the price of the target company's shares rises. The premium paid in these situations varies considerably and inevitably depends on the circumstances but 20–50 per cent is not unusual. It could be considerably higher where there is, for example, more than one predator, or might be lower if, for instance, the company's price is already buoyed up because of takeover proposals. The usefulness of the comparisons will inevitably depend on the information available and the closeness of the comparison.

Where the comparable company's shares are traded on the Stock Exchange, it is likely that the information available about the sale and the target company's trading record and prospects will be quite detailed. On the other hand, the information available to a purchaser of an unquoted company will be treated as confidential and that available to the valuer is almost always limited. In any event unless a prophet, he will not know what was in the purchaser's mind. To place undue reliance on a sale price when the full circumstances of the transaction, and in particular the information available, are unknown can be extremely dangerous. For example, say a company's historic trading record indicates an upward trend culminating in profits before tax in the latest published accounts of £200,000 and the purchase price is £1 million. This represents an historic pre-tax multiple of five and so the valuer assumes that for a company with a similar trading record, and comparable in all other respects, a reasonable historic pre-tax multiple would be five. Unknown to him the company was forecasting a reduction in profits before tax to £100,000 because of the loss of key personnel, and the sale price therefore represented a prospective pre-tax multiple of 10. The valuer adopting the historic multiple of five would do so on an entirely misconceived basis and his valuation could be inaccurate by as much as 100 per cent.

Analogous companies must be checked to see whether they are comparable with the company to be valued. As far as possible like should be compared with like. In particular, growth prospects, nature of business, size and status (listed or unlisted) should be similar to the company under consideration. Ideally the companies will be similar in all respects. In practice, the valuer invariably needs to consider less than ideal comparisons and the multiple he adopts must make allowance for any differences. Adjustments must be made on the basis of common sense and experience.

Another way of arriving at a capitalisation factor is to ascertain the cost of borrowing to purchase the company. As an example, the cost of borrowing might be, say, 2 or 3 per cent above current minimum lending rate or base rate. The normal lender, e.g. a bank, will not presumably take a greater risk than a potential purchaser and a premium is therefore added to take this into account. Let us take an example. The expected interest rate on borrowed funds is 12½ per cent and the target company's maintainable after-tax earnings are considered to be £10,000. If the purchase price is £80,000, the whole of the profit will be taken up in interest payments. A value of £80,000 is therefore too high and a lower multiple appropriate.

This approach is useful because it can highlight the position for an individual purchaser, who knows the likely cost of borrowing and the returns that can be expected from other forms of investment and can consequently judge whether the expected return justifies the risk. The disadvantage is that the market may include many other prospective purchasers with different requirements and expectations. The valuer needs to be aware of the prices they are likely to pay as the market generally will determine the value of the company.

Although practitioners may find the biggest problem with the use of comparable companies is the absence of detailed information, nevertheless the prices paid in actual transactions provide the best guide to prices in the market. There is a relationship between returns on other forms of investments such as gilts, bank deposit or building society accounts, but the closer the comparison the smaller the adjustment for any differences and the less arbitrary the valuation.

The assets basis of valuation

The term 'assets basis' is used here to describe valuation by reference to assets. There is not one assets basis of valuation but two bases; the investment basis and the break-up basis.

The investment basis

The investment basis approach to valuation applies mainly to property investment and investment holding companies. Valuation of these companies will usually be based on the value of the assets on a going concern basis, because the purchaser is interested primarily in capital appreciation. The intermediate income is of secondary importance. Unless there is a special reason to wind up the company or dispose of its investments in the immediate future, the value of these companies will be related to the value of the underlying assets.

Care must be taken to obtain the current market value of individual assets and it is often essential to obtain the advice of specialist valuers for items such as freehold property.

The most common problem is likely to be contingent Corporation Tax arising on the revaluation of assets. Where it is not expected that the assets will be sold in the immediate future, a full deduction for Corporation Tax on any revaluation surplus should not be made from the company's assets. The actual allowance depends on the circumstances but in the common situation where the majority of the assets are expected to be held for many years, the contingent tax liability will be substantially discounted. On the other hand, if the contingent liability is expected to crystallise in the near future, the full liability or a substantial part thereof should be deducted. Realisation costs should be treated in the same manner.

The break-up basis

The break-up basis of valuation is appropriate where the value of a trading company as a going concern by reference to earnings indicates a lower value than would be expected if the company's assets were sold or the business wound up. In essence the company has become uneconomical and it makes commercial sense to cease trading and realise the company's assets. A break-up value is a minimum value.

The assets of a company are generally shown in its accounts at historic cost or the lower of cost or net realisable value. In practice the book value in the accounts sometimes bears little relation to the current market value. Freehold and leasehold property purchased many years earlier will presumably have appreciated in value; plant and machinery may have a higher second-hand value or only a scrap value; stocks and work in progress may need to be substantially discounted for a quick sale.

An estimate of realisation costs must also be made. These might consist of liquidator's fees, estate agent's fees and redundancy compensation. If the company is run down slowly, so as perhaps to maximise the value of the work in progress, there could be substantial overhead costs during the winding-up period to take into account. In total, the costs are often considerable and usually the value of the company will be greater on a going-concern basis.

Finally, a purchaser will require a return or profit on his investment. This will need to reflect the uncertainties, risk and the delay in distributions. The valuer must be careful though not to discount twice for these factors. For example, if the stock has been discounted to allow for losses which would be incurred on a sale at an auction and the written-down value is a realistic estimate, a further discount for the risk or uncertainty is unwarranted.

The significance of assets in valuation

The occasions when a valuation will be arrived at on the basis of assets have been mentioned. This does not mean that assets are irrelevant in all other circumstances. Many practitioners believe that assets reassure a purchaser and a strong asset backing can be used to support a higher value on a capitalisation of earnings approach. There is no hard-and-fast rule: it must depend on the facts. Certainly, if two companies are identical except for their asset backing, a purchaser might reasonably pay more for the company with the higher asset backing. However generally, the assets of trading companies are principally of importance only in so far as they affect profits. For example, if the plant and machinery is in good condition, or a property is ideally situated, then the condition and position should be reflected in the estimation of maintainable earnings.

Of course, if the company's assets are not used for the purposes of its trading activities and can be treated as investments, they will need to be valued separately. For example, company A's assets consist of:

	£
Freehold property	1,000
Investments	2,000
Net current assets	4,000
Total	7,000

Company A's profits may be subdivided as follows:

	£
Profits from trading activities	1,000
Income from investments	200
Total	1,200

Let us assume that the valuer has satisfied himself that the investments are not required to support its trading activities and arrived at a pre-tax profit multiple of five. The company's value is £7,000, that is five years' purchase of its profits of £1,000 from trading activities plus the value of £2,000 for its investments.

Other bases of valuation

The principal methods of valuation are the earnings and assets bases described. There are other methods, some of which are merely, in the author's opinion, derivatives of the earnings basis: the super-profits and discounted cashflow techniques, and trade practices.

The super-profits approach

This is used to value goodwill, that is the difference between the going concern value of a company as a whole and the value of its net tangible assets.

To calculate the value of a company on this basis it is necessary to ascertain the market value of the tangible assets and ascertain a reasonable rate of return. The resulting figure is deducted from maintainable profits to arrive at what are known as super-profits. The super-profits are then capitalised by a suitable multiple to arrive at the value for goodwill. The value of the company is the combined value of goodwill and its separable net assets.

Example:

	£
Profit after tax	300,000
Interest on capital employed, say 15% on £1.5 million	225,000
Super-profits	75,000
Capitalisation factor say 3	225,000
Add back net tangible assets	1,500,000
Value of company	1,725,000

The difficulties of estimating market values for the company's tangible assets and the arbitrary nature of the capitalisation factor makes the valuation by reference to super-profits far from satisfactory. As a method it appears to be losing favour and the author can see no advantage of this method over the normal capitalisation of earnings approach. Indeed, ascertaining an appropriate multiple to super-profits is fraught with difficulties in view of the shortage, or even absence, of reliable comparable transactions. The approach was criticised and dismissed in the case of *Buckingham* v. *Francis*.

Discounted cashflow

The theory behind this method of valuation is that the value of a business reflects the present value of its future cashflows. An estimate is made of the amount and timing of the cashflows and a discount rate applied to them to arrive at the present value.

The cashflows are after-tax profits plus non-cash charges to income (for example depreciation) *less* future capital expenditure. The rate of discount is an appropriate interest rate factor.

Example:

	Projected cashflow	Discount factor at say 20%	Present value
Year 1	100,000	0.8333333	83,333
2	200,000	0.6944444	138,889
3	250,000	0.5787037	144,676
4	300,000	0.4822531	144,676
5	400,000	0.4018776	160,751
		Present value	672,325

For the purposes of the above example five years' cashflows have been used. A longer period could be adopted if considered desirable.

Because the company would normally continue trading, or have some value on a winding up, it is necessary to add a residual value to the figure of £672,325 to arrive at the value of the company as a whole. This might either be the estimated break-up value at the end of year 5 or a calculation of the present value of the business, *ad infinitum*. For simplicity's sake, if it is assumed the company will wind up at the end of year 5 with a realisable value of £1 million, the present value of the company will be £1,074,202, that is £672,325 plus £1 million discounted at the discount rate for year 5 of 0.4018776.

As a mathematical approach, on first sight the discounted cashflow approach seems less subjective than the capitalisation of profits method of valuation. However, the interest rate factor is no less, and possibly more, arbitrary than capitalisation multiples. Furthermore, the accuracy of any cashflows more than a couple of years into the future is debatable. It is perhaps not surprising that the method tends to be used for valuing capital projects rather than for valuing companies.

Trade practices

Certain businesses are considered to have special trade practices. For example, the value of bookmakers and casinos are sometimes calculated as a multiple of turnover, while professional practices are sometimes advertised at a value representing a multiple of fees. Ultimately, the value of such companies should relate to their profit-earning capability and generally any value on such a basis which cannot be substantiated by reference to earnings must be treated with suspicion.

There are some exceptions to this general rule. Some businesses may be purchased for their name, prestige or influence. For example, it could be argued that some football clubs are bought for reasons other than profits. They often make losses and, because of planning restrictions, cannot usually hope to realise a profit on the sale of the ground. Loss-making newspapers change hands at values in excess of their net tangible asset backing. The value placed on these types of company can only be judged on the particular circumstances and the likely purchasers in the market at any particular time. In other words, value is in the eye of the beholder, and a company may well be worth more to one purchaser than another.

Acquisition and merger accounting

This chapter has been confined to methods of financial evaluation and has not covered all the factors which influence the value of a company. As well as examining the historic results and future prospects of the company the valuer should also consider the following factors:

1. business activities and market profile,
2. management effectiveness and succession,
3. financial status (gearing, liquidity, assets),
4. takeover or flotation prospects.

There is one other factor which needs to be specifically addressed and that is the implications of acquisition and merger accounting.

Prima facie the accounting policies of a company which is to be valued should not affect the value arrived at. A valuer will, however, need to research carefully the policies adopted by the company and make any adjustments to the company's declared profit considered appropriate before applying the earnings multiple. For an acquiring company this will probably mean calculating the effect on the target company's profits of bringing that company's accounting policies into line with its own.

The method that a purchasing company itself is going to use to account for the business combination will also affect the value that it is prepared to pay for its target. The choice is first between acquisition accounting and, if permitted, merger accounting. Consideration of this includes the related availability (or not) of merger relief under the Companies Act 1985. Secondly, if acquisition accounting is adopted, the purchaser must decide how any goodwill arising on consolidation is to be eliminated.

The subject of accounting for business combinations is complex, and both the accounting standards and the law relating to the topic are likely to change before the end of the 1980s. These amendments are likely to narrow the circumstances in which merger accounting is permitted and limit the choice of methods available for eliminating goodwill from the consolidated accounts of an acquiring company. In view of the impending changes, however, anything said here must be treated as relevant at the time of writing only (1988).

Presently available practices can and do affect the amounts paid for companies, and therefore their values, by affecting the ability of the purchaser to pay the price with minimal adverse effect on the purchaser's own accounts. The critical factor is the ability to merger account, or if not, at least to obtain merger relief under the provisions of the Companies Act.

For readers not familiar with the difference between acquisition accounting and merger accounting, the following example may help to show some of the principal contrasting effects of the two methods:

Company A has bought company B at 31 December by issuing 90 shares with a market value of £3 per share. The fair value of the assets of company B at 31 December is £250. Both companies' accounts are drawn up at 31 December each year. Prior to the acquisition/merger the balance sheets of the two companies show:

	A Ltd £	B Ltd £
Net assets	220	190
£1 ordinary shares	100	90
Profit and loss account	120	100
	£220	£190

The balance sheet of A Ltd after the transaction, according to each of the two methods shows:

	Acquisition method £	Merger method £
Previous net assets	220	220
Investment in B Ltd	270	90
	£490	£310
£1 ordinary shares	190	190
Share premium account	180	—
Profit and loss account	120	120
	£490	£310

The consolidated balance sheet of A Ltd after the transaction, according to each of the two methods above:

	Acquisition method £	Merger method £
Net assets	470	410
Goodwill	20	—
	£490	£410
£1 ordinary shares	190	190
Share premium account	180	—
Profit and loss account	120	220
	£490	£410

It can be seen from the above example that merger accounting, as opposed to acquisition accounting:

1. avoids the recording of goodwill on acquisition and therefore the need either to write it off against reserves or to amortise it against future profits;
2. maintains in the consolidated accounts the previous depreciation charge on the fixed assets of the acquired company rather than having to charge depreciation on the value of those assets as revalued at the date of acquisition;
3. leaves the pre-acquisition profits of the new subsidiary available for distribution to the new owner by restricting the recorded cost of the new investment to the par value of the shares issued; and

4. requires the consolidated accounts in the year of acquisition to include a full year's trading for the new subsidiary and not just the results from the date of acquisition.

As significant cash does not leave the acquiring company, the consideration being required to be at least 90 per cent in shares, all these benefits imply that the purchaser who can merger account will be able to show higher profits both in the year of acquisition and in later years, and therefore may be able to afford to pay more than one which cannot merger account.

Merger relief under the Companies Act, which must be available for merger accounting to be permissible, also provides one significant advantage to the purchasing company even if merger accounting is ruled out. Acquisition accounting with merger relief escapes the company law requirement to record a share premium account. This either avoids the recording of goodwill or provides a reserve against which it can be eliminated or substantially reduced without recourse to the courts. Again, this may tempt the purchaser to pay more than would be the case were there to be commitment to a future charge against profits for amortising goodwill.

By avoiding or minimising the adverse accounting consequences of accounting for a business combination, particularly the amortisation or write-off of goodwill, the higher depreciation charge and the freezing of pre-acquisition profits, purchasing companies have been able or tempted to increase the price offered for a target company. Hence we have heard complaints from the United States that UK companies are able to outbid their US rivals for US targets because UK purchasers either have no problem with goodwill because they can merger account or do not have to amortise the goodwill arising on the acquisition because they can write it off against reserves. On the other side of the coin, however, companies in countries where goodwill can be carried on the balance sheet, or where consolidated accounts are not required, have an advantage over UK companies in a competitive auction as the penalty for increasing the purchase price is less onerous to them.

The conclusion is that the accounting policies available to purchasers do affect the price they are prepared to pay for a company which is, after all, the ultimate test of that company's value.

Financing acquisitions

The decision as to how an acquisition should be financed can be affected by many factors. There are three basic types of finance that are available – shares, cash or loan stock – and they can be used alone or in combination.

In recent years, companies and their bankers have been highly imaginative in creating new financial instruments (such as convertible loan stock and convertible preference shares) that combine some or all of the features of the basic types of consideration, or enable vendors (and buyers) to choose between them either when the deal is done or at a later date. The most important factors in deciding how an acquisition should be financed can be grouped into a number of categories, as follows:

1. *Terms of the deal*

   The method of financing an acquisition is determined to a very large extent by what the vendor is prepared to accept and on what terms the deal has been agreed. Nevertheless, some flexibility may be available. For example, if an acquisition has been agreed as a cash transaction, it may well be possible to persuade the vendor to take shares, providing that it is possible to guarantee that those shares can be sold in the market for an equivalent consideration, typically through a placing. This type of 'vendor placing' can combine the advantages of a cash transaction for the vendor with those of a share transaction for the acquirer. It is more important, in reaching agreement with the vendor, to have a clear view of how an acquisition is to be financed and to have the details clearly spelt out in the purchase contract, including the responsibility for costs.

2. *The timing of the payment of the consideration*

   Consideration may be payable either at completion or on deferred terms. If deferred consideration is payable in cash, care should be taken to ensure that when that consideration becomes payable the cost of finance has not risen to unacceptably high levels through changes in interest and exchange rates. If deferred consideration is in the form of shares, then the number of shares to be issued is likely to vary with the share price. If the share price falls between agreement of the deal and the issue of shares, an issue of an unacceptably high number of shares may have a significant effect on earnings per share and even on the control position of the purchaser. It may be possible to acquire an option, whereby the company is able to sell its own shares at a fixed price on the date for the issue of shares as settlement of the consideration. This process involves legal complications and should not be considered without taking professional advice beforehand but can provide useful protection against undue dilution. Often, deferred consideration is related to the future profitability of the business being acquired, which can give rise to additional financing considerations. In particular, the effect of future costs on the overall levels of gearing and the treatment of goodwill arising from payments of deferred consideration need careful planning in advance.

3. *If the consideration is to be shares*

   If a company issues shares as consideration for an acquisition there are a number of important matters to be taken into account. The issue of those new shares will affect the earnings per share of the acquiring company, and thus its market valuation. While it is normally acceptable for earnings to be diluted for perhaps a year following a significant acquisition, dilution over a longer period is generally considered to be detrimental to the market's perception of a company. It may be possible to take advantage of merger relief, thus maximising the reserves available for distribution. If this is the case then it becomes possible to write off any goodwill arising from that acquisition against the share premium arising from the issue of the shares used as consideration. This eliminates the need to amortise goodwill against future profits, and can significantly increase future earnings. The use of the vendor placing technique mentioned above can provide an opportunity both to be able to use merger relief and write off goodwill from the outset while providing the vendor with cash consideration.

   If a placing of shares is to be undertaken, either for the company to raise cash for an acquisition, or on behalf of the vendor, the effect on the market price of the company's shares of the placing must be carefully considered. As well as ensuring that the shares can actually be placed, there may be an opportunity to introduce 'friendly institutions' as shareholders or to improve the spread of equity investors in order to promote the company's long-term aims and ambitions.

4. *If the consideration is to be cash*

   The vast majority of acquisitions made by companies are paid for in cash. In most cases the issue of loan stock can be considered as analogous to cash, unless the vendors can be persuaded to accept loan stock which is unsecured. If they can be so persuaded, then this leaves more security available for the banks and other financiers than would otherwise be the case, and may then increase the total borrowings that can be raised. If the acquisition is to be financed using borrowed monies, it is, of course, most important to consider the costs of this finance and reduce its sensitivity to changes in interest rates as far as possible. Fixed rate loans can be raised, funds can be swapped, or an interest rate cap or a similar hedging instrument can be purchased to achieve this result. These instruments are now available to cover borrowings as small as £500,000 and can offer a cheap and effective way for a company to control increases in its interest costs while still being able to enjoy the benefits of falls in rates.

   It is also necessary to consider which legal entity should make the borrowings.

Different legal entities within a group may be subject to different tax regimes, or may be able to raise money at substantially lower cost than other members of the group. For example, it may be that a particular company in the group is able to provide a natural currency hedge (perhaps through its sales income) against borrowings in a currency such as the German mark, which carries low interest rates. Thus, that entity can make borrowings at low interest rates without the need for expensive external hedging of the currency. Unless there are natural currency hedges in the group, it is important that exposures to changes in currency exchange rates are minimised by ensuring borrowings are taken up in the same currency as that which will be used to service them. It is also important that borrowings are raised in the same currency as the assets which they are to finance, to prevent a balance sheet exposure to currency fluctuations. Occasionally, the cashflows which are to be used to service the borrowings are not the same as those in which the assets are denominated. There is a wide range of techniques available to hedge exposures such as these, but it is not within the scope of this book to examine them in detail. However, it is important that these issues are addressed at the outset and that appropriate measures are taken within the context of the treasury and exchange risk management policy of the acquiring company.

Another point to consider is the effect that the borrowings will have on the credit rating of the combined entity. It will be necessary to compare the post-acquisition debt–equity ratio to that of other companies operating in the same sector, and to review and compare the number of times interest and debt service costs will be covered by profits before interest and taxation. The level of security available to borrowers will also have to be considered.

5. *Taxation considerations*
The method of financing an acquisition will be affected by a taxation consideration of both the acquirer and the vendor. These are dealt with elsewhere in this book, but they are of critical importance and should be carefully considered at the outset.

6. *Other points to consider*
It may be possible for the form of finance for an acquisition to be used to serve an additional purpose. For example, it may be possible to use shares as a continuing incentive to employee shareholders in the target business, or to raise borrowings in a currency which provides a natural hedge to exposures in other parts of the business. When an acquisition is made, it is normally an opportunity to review the financing of the whole of the combined operation to take advantage of any opportunities that may arise.

7. *Leveraged acquisitions*

Recently, banks have been prepared to lend very considerably more than they have previously to enable companies to make acquisitions. In part, this is because companies are now able, in certain circumstances, to provide assistance for the acquisition of their own shares. A company can therefore sometimes use the assets and cashflow of the company it is buying to finance the cost of its acquisition. Competition between banks has contributed to this more aggressive approach, and some banks are prepared to lend based on the cashflow of acquisition targets, above and beyond the lending that the security available to the bank might otherwise justify. Naturally, this type of borrowing is expensive and the banks often require an option over a part of the acquiring company's share capital as an additional reward.

The US junk-bond market has enabled many companies to finance acquisitions using borrowed monies to a much greater extent than had previously been thought possible. The first few European junk-bond issues are being planned at present. These bonds are issued at interest rates substantially higher than those that might otherwise be obtained, reflecting the greater risks being taken by investors.

8. *Conclusion*

There are no hard and fast rules as to how to finance acquisitions. The terms in which banks are prepared to lend money vary continuously, as do the terms in which loan stock and shares can be issued. Professional advice and the advice of bankers and stockbrokers should be taken whenever a significant acquisition is to be financed.

Chapter 4

Evaluating companies for
:acquisition

JONATHAN F. TAYLOR

Chief Executive, Booker

and

JOHN DEWHURST

Acquisitions Manager, ICI

Introduction

In evaluating any acquisition possibility there are many important aspects
to be taken into account. By far the most important of these is *strategic
relevance*. It may be that the purchase of one company by another without
too much thought or forward planning is successful. However, this is a
matter of luck and with the sums of money which have to be paid to
acquire good companies, you would have to be foolish to rely on luck
rather than professional competence.

Reference is made in other chapters of this book to the importance of
strategy in the acquisition process. The conclusion is always the same –
the best guarantee of success is to set out a clear strategy and from this
to decide which type of company should be acquired and what strategic
objectives it should satisfy.

Of course, there will be more than one company that will meet these
strategic objectives, so how is the choice made between alternatives? The
answer rests on value for money and this, in turn, depends on the synergy
which can be obtained from an acquisition. Synergy is an all-embracing
term, difficult to define precisely and often misused. Essentially it refers
to the total of additional financial benefits which a company expects to
obtain from an acquisition. These may be cost-savings from rationalisation
of production or distribution, or from extra sales through the existing
marketing staff, or from enhanced and complementary research and
development or, indeed, from a myriad of other items.

In order to calculate synergy it is important to have the fullest and most
accurate information about the company which is to be acquired. Later
in this chapter the ways in which such information can be obtained are

reviewed. Accurate financial information is clearly important, not least to determine the stand-alone value, i.e. the value of a company before any allowance is made for the extra benefits coming from synergy.

Some of the non-financial areas which require careful review prior to acquisition are fairly obvious. How strong is the market position? How wide/robust is the product range? How useful is the research and development? Other areas, however, may be less obvious and more difficult to assess. Human resource is one such difficult area. How good is the management team? How competent is the sales force? Though more difficult to evaluate, this is crucial in determining the success or otherwise of an acquisition.

A further important aspect of evaluation is to look for the hidden downsides. In the financial area, for example, it is important to understand fully the accounting conventions used and to check the adequacy of funding of, say, the pension fund. The state of equipment and facilities should be reviewed to ensure that maintenance expenditure has been at an appropriate level. The legality of patents and the relevance of pending litigation are all potential traps which could necessitate extra expenditure post-acquisition or weaken financial viability.

The remainder of this chapter illustrates the approach and experience of two companies which have been very active in the M & A area – Booker and ICI. There are many basic lessons to be learned from their experience. However, there are also new lessons which these companies, along with others, will continue to learn since acquisitions is a developing and changing world.

The Booker story

Introduction

Arguably the successful identification, evaluation and implementation of acquisitions is as much an art as a science, and even the most sophisticated analysis will not take sufficient account of the human resources and dynamics of a business. As Professor Michael Porter and others warn us, both sides of the Atlantic are littered with unsuccessful mergers and acquisitions. Our track record in Booker seems to have been quite good and this probably reflects a combination of luck, sound evaluation processes and a concern with the human dimension.

Over the last four years, since I became chief executive of Booker, we have made 25 acquisitions and six divestments. In the same period our pre-tax profit has grown at a compound annual rate of 27 per cent and our earnings per share at a rate of 28 per cent. Much of this growth has been organic from within the company, but carefully chosen small and medium-sized acquisitions have also been important contributors. We have not been one of those companies which has grown on the back of very large transactions, often financed by the issue of shares and often facilitated by rather 'cosmetic' accounting practices, and whose further growth may depend on a further mega-deal.

Sources of acquisitions

Our acquisitions seem to come from three main sources:

1. Small publicly-quoted companies, often with a single large share-holding group. Examples include Sharpes (seeds), Daehnfeldt (seeds in Denmark), and Whitworth (distribution of fresh produce).
2. Subsidiaries of larger public companies which are rationalising their own businesses. In our case, examples of such acquisitions have been: Atlantic Sea Products (salmon farming) from Bartz-Johannessen, Nature's Best (health food) from Guinness, Country Kitchen Foods (mushrooms) from Heinz, Eversheds (delivered food distribution) from Hillsdown and Linfood (cash and carry) from Gateway.
3. Privately-owned companies such as Hursts (seeds), McNabs (cash and carry), Middlebrook (mushrooms) and Loseley (dairy products).

But in each case our method of evaluation, which I discuss later in this chapter, is similar, with the human dimension always of the greatest importance. It is also worth noting that our acquisitions have always been made on a friendly, rather than hostile, basis.

To understand our method of evaluation it is perhaps helpful to understand something of our company. Booker operates on a very decentralised basis, with authority and responsibility delegated to its main divisions and to profit centres within those divisions. At the same time, there is a framework of strong financial discipline which ensures a proper control of cash usage and a full understanding of the performance of individual businesses in the context of agreed budgets and longer term plans. But we do not try to make operating decisions from the centre nor to second-guess operating management. The latter is accountable for profit and must have the authority necessary to make good that accountability. A number of consequences flow from such a decentralised structure.

First, there is a very small head office. A team of 14 executives and professionals looks after a business with sales in excess of £2 billion. Many of the head office executives are concerned with the functions of financial control, treasury and tax.

Second, in evaluating acquisitions we rely heavily on the skills and resources of our own operating businesses, supplemented by a limited availability of head office staff and, on appropriate occasions, consultants.

Third, our businesses tend to retain their separate identities, names and cultures. This becomes a positive advantage when acquiring a business with a long proud history which does not wish to be submerged in a corporate giant.

Fourth, we have no great reserves of centrally-based corporate management on which to draw and inject into new acquisitions. The quality of existing management, and its compatibility with our own people, is therefore very important.

Synergy, strategy and simplicity

An acquisition candidate, whether identified by the corporate centre or by one of our operating businesses or brought to us by an investment bank or other specialist intermediary, will have to satisfy three requirements:

1. *Synergy.* This overused word is useful shorthand for quantifiable merger benefits: that two and two should make five, or preferably six. I shall discuss what is meant in greater detail later in the chapter.
2. *Strategy.* We take great pride that almost all our businesses are in leading positions in markets that are growing (although some of those markets are still relatively small). An acquisition should reinforce such positions.
3. *Simplicity.* The easiest acquisition is one which fits straight alongside an existing business and does not involve massive reorganisation or restructuring.

When all is said and done, the fundamental requirement for a successful acquisition is that it should add value; that is to say, the value of the merged businesses must be greater than that of the two separate businesses added together. Value, as far as we are concerned, must inevitably be measured in terms of profitability and cash generation. There are many ways in which the combination of two businesses can add value.

Adding value

I do not intend discussing the evaluation of acquisitions which are primarily 'asset situations'. These are the speciality of such conglomerates as Hanson and BTR and involve acquiring businesses which are basically sound, albeit often mature, but are under-performing for one reason or another, and are therefore under-valued. They represent a legitimate way to add value but there are not many left and a pure 'asset situation' will never be a primary target as far as Booker is concerned. That is not to say, however, that we are not extremely interested in assets and will be looking for ways to make them work harder or, in appropriate circumstances, be disposing of those which are surplus to our needs or do not fit.

Generally, our acquisitions are strategic in nature and involve businesses which are concerned with markets and products where we already have some presence. In very happy circumstances, an acquisition may be almost identical to one of our own businesses. The synergy from the combination will include the cost savings available from putting together production, distribution, research and development and marketing, financial and general management functions. Margins may be improved further because of the reduced competition implicit in the combination of two existing players or through the enhanced buying power of an enlarged business.

Where the markets and products are complementary, rather than identical, there are synergies in terms of the broadening of the markets served by each product group and an increase in the product range supported by the combined marketing and research and development effort. Again, there is likely to be scope for reduced management, distribution and marketing costs and more cost-effective research and development expenditure in the combined business.

We have, of course, to be certain that the management expertise is available to run the combined operation effectively following an acquisition. We may have, within our own businesses, the capacity to manage the enlarged operation and to secure the anticipated cost savings and revenue benefits of the merger during a period in which there is bound to be considerable uncertainty for all employees. Alternatively, the acquisition may bring with it high-calibre management capable, under appropriate direction, of securing the merger benefits. Incentives such as performance bonuses, profit-related pay and share options all have their place in this process. Disaster awaits any acquirer which can see the potential synergies arising from a takeover but which does not have the management available to realise them.

A type of acquisition with which Booker has had considerable success is the small, usually family-owned, business on the verge of transition to something more substantial. The owners and entrepreneurs involved will usually have great knowledge of their markets and great skill in serving them. Management will, however, often be 'seat of the pants' in style and this may work well enough in a business small enough for the owner/managers to know in detail what is going on in every part of it. It is a style, however, which often fails in the transition to becoming a more substantial enterprise. In such cases we can provide the existing owners with a means of realising their capital while adding financial backing, management accounting systems and controls and market expertise and leverage. The clever bit is to do this without adding a layer of bureaucracy and costs and without decreasing the motivation of the existing owner/managers whose experience and skills are still critical for success. Leaving management with a minority stake or basing the purchase price on a formula linked to future profitability can help ensure the continued and fully committed involvement of the key personnel. An initial minority stake may also be appropriate where the owners are reluctant to lose control immediately. It will be essential in such cases for a shareholders' agreement to be negotiated covering, *inter alia*, board representation, management issues, strategic development and capital expenditure, dividend policy and, most importantly, an option to secure a controlling interest in appropriate circumstances.

Cashflow – the acid test

As I have already emphasised, the added value of an acquisition must be demonstrable as an increase in the profit and cashflow attributable to our shareholders. The acid test is cashflow. Many of the costs involved in the integration of two businesses may well be reflected in a goodwill write-off for accounting purposes and so have little impact on profitability; but they still represent an outflow of real value as far as our shareholders are concerned. Profitability, which is not ultimately available to shareholders as cash for either distribution or reinvestment, is of little value. Hence, our evaluation process will always include some form of discounted cashflow (DCF) analysis.

This analysis will involve the preparation of a plan for the combined business for, say, ten years from the acquisition date and identifying the cash outflows, including the purchase price, and cash inflows which will result over and above those which might be expected from our existing business. The cash inflows and outflows for each year are then discounted back to their value at the time of acquisition using a predetermined discount rate. The discount rate chosen will represent our minimum acceptable return on capital; we call it the 'hurdle rate'. The discounted cashflows are then added together to arrive at the net present value of the acquisition. Any positive value indicates that the acquisition will earn the necessary minimum return on investment and the higher the value the greater the return for our shareholders. If there is a choice of possible acquisitions, which are simple to implement and fit strategically, we prefer the one showing the highest net present value. There are, however, a number of problems in this type of analysis.

First, it is difficult to make even half-realistic projections for a ten-year period, particularly when one's knowledge of the potential acquisition may be limited. There is no way around this problem. It is thus unrealistic to build in to forecasts the continuing market and market share growth and cost savings which tend to characterise the initial post-acquisition period.

Second, it is necessary to calculate a residual value for the business at the end of the discount period. Given adequate asset replacement and long-term marketing expenditure, the business should be worth at least the initial purchase price plus the amount of new investment. Another possibility is to value the business at a multiple of the final year's forecast cashflows. In any event, an estimate of the residual value must be included in the forecast as the final year's cash inflow.

Third, it is necessary to determine whether inflation should be included in the forecast. We usually show all cashflows in current value terms and use a real discount rate (i.e. a rate excluding inflationary expectations) to discount those flows. However, others may find it easier to assess viability in terms of a discount rate which incorporates inflationary expectations and is, therefore, comparable to interest rates.

The final, and most difficult, problem is where to set the hurdle rate. A realistic approach is to start with an estimate of our cost of funds. To this must then be added a premium which will vary with the risk perceived in the proposed acquisition. An acquisition will usually be more risky than the capital investments undertaken in our existing business on a day-to-day basis and so could be expected to require a higher premium over cost of funds.

Our cost of funds will again be the subject of a number of considerations. What balance between equity and debt financing should be assumed for any given acquisition? If one acquisition is financed by debt, the next may have to be financed by an equity issue; should the second acquisition evaluation be penalised with a higher hurdle rate? The most practical method is probably to set an agreed target mix of funding between debt and equity and set a hurdle rate based on an agreed mix of debt and equity.

In addition to calculating the net present value from a discounted cashflow, we calculate the internal rate of return of the cashflow. This gives us a rate of return which can then be measured against the hurdle rate and the rates of return on other investment proposals.

We also look at the payback period for a proposed acquisition. This measures the length of time taken for the investment to recover the initial purchase price out of future cash generation. In the case of long-term strategic investments, we give less weight to this particular measure. The return on capital employed forecast to be earned at various points in the future is of greater concern. But how long an investment should take to earn an acceptable return on assets, and what represents an acceptable return will be the subject of debate in each particular case.

Finally, we want to know when the proposed acquisition will increase profit before taxation and earnings per share, and the likely size of those increases. Although we pride ourselves on making long-term investment decisions, we are, none the less, also concerned whether an investment will enhance, or dilute, earnings in the shorter term.

The financial analysis of an acquisition is, of course, only as good as the data and the judgements on which it is based. The collection of data – on costs, markets, products, management and the workforce, physical assets and all the rest – is a lengthy and time-consuming process. Some of the information will come from sources which are publicly available and some, where the transaction is amicable, will come from the management of the business itself. In Appendix A the sort of information which can be gleaned from public sources is presented.

The ICI experience

Introduction

The chapter so far has concentrated on acquisitions of small or medium-sized companies. At the other end of the spectrum are acquisitions of large companies. These are not different in kind but bring with them certain additional features and complexities, some of which have relevant lessons for all types of acquisitions. Large acquisitions are normally made by large companies with appropriate financial resources, although there have been some examples in the recent past of relatively small companies over capitalising in order to make purchases of quite large companies.

Many features of the purchase of large companies by large companies are extremely similar to those described in the earlier part of this chapter, although there are also some significant differences. One company which has been very active in the acquisitions field over the last few years is ICI. It is intended to use this company as an example of how a large company carries out acquisitions, mergers and divestment activities and draw some parallels and some new lessons from such activities.

Like Booker, ICI operates with a small corporate acquisitions team of approximately five people. This small group is responsible for coordinating all effort throughout the world in the acquisitions area. ICI also draws on internal expertise and resources to a very large extent. All acquisitions involve from the outset heavy involvement by the appropriate business, which will ultimately carry the responsibility for the future management of the newly acquired company.

All successful acquisitions require a clearly defined company strategy and acquisitions objectives. In this respect ICI is no exception. Equally, in order to be successful for the purchasing company, the acquisition must contain significant synergies. The elements of synergy have been defined and described earlier in this chapter. However, it is clearly important with a larger transaction, and hence a more expensive transaction, that the synergies are not only adequate but robust. It is a fairly simple matter to list the theoretical cost improvements which might be generated by acquisition. What is important is to test absolutely and independently whether or not these synergies can genuinely be achieved.

Moreover, it is important not to give away all the synergy benefit in the purchase price. If a company has a market value of £500 million and the acquiring company believes there is synergy of £200 million, this might appear to justify a purchase price of £700 million. However, if a full price of £700 million is paid, what benefits remain to the purchasing company since it will have given away all the benefits to the seller?

Features of large acquisitions

What are the features of a large acquisition, which in some ways may be different from a small or medium-sized acquisition? First, the company is more likely to be a public company. The full implications of this are referred to later in the book, but essentially they relate to the need to meet stockholder and Stock Exchange requirements in whichever country in the world the company is purchased. Valuation methods used for large transactions are similar to smaller transactions. However, it is more likely that not all of the acquired company will be retained. It is therefore necessary not only to ascribe a purchase value to the proposed acquisition, but also to form a view at an early stage on the possible divestment value of those pieces which will not be retained.

Large acquisition possibilities are normally generally known to be available. There is, therefore, open competition and hence the expectation that perhaps it will be necessary to pay a higher price than with private transactions. It is more likely that external financial advisers will be used in such transactions, at least to participate in the valuation process.

The most actively developed acquisitions market is that of the United States. Although practices are different from the UK and other countries, it is perhaps useful to look at examples of a US-based acquisition in order to understand the full complexities and intricacies of a large deal for a public company in an auction or competitive process. The way in which the process works in ICI is as follows.

Strategic review

On a regular basis the strategies of the individual businesses within the company are reviewed. This strategic review covers future performance in the coming years and leads on to strategic direction over the next few years. It will cover such topics as technology, requirements for capital expenditure, geographical and product diversification and acquisition or divestment requirements. Once the strategy has been presented by the business, reviewed by the Board and agreed, those elements which relate to acquisitions are passed to the corporate acquisitions team.

This team is continually reviewing and monitoring companies which might be available for acquisition. It attempts to match the requirements as defined by this strategy with companies which exist today. At this point in time it may not be known or apparent that a company is or might be up for sale. However, all public data relating to that company are collected and catalogued. Each internal business which might have an interest in that company is then asked to produce its own business report. This is continually updated together with market intelligence gathered from the investment banking and merchant banking community.

An important part of acquisitions activity is having eyes and ears in the marketplace. Every resource, internal and external to the company, is used on a continuous basis to monitor and gather information. Through this process it is hoped that the company will learn at an early stage that a target company has in fact become available. For purposes of this example I intend to examine the situation where a large public corporation declares it will sell off the whole or a major part of the business and proposes to go down an auction route.

The auction process

Once this fact becomes known, the acquisitions group of the company, together with the relevant businesses, produces the latest update on that company. This is then presented to the Board of the company with a total picture, as clearly as can be known, about the target company. Even at this stage a price indication is given using the types of valuation method described in other parts of this book. Any known areas of difficulty, for example, prospective problems around the pension fund or liabilities or loans would also be highlighted at this early stage. The Board will then be asked to give the go-ahead for the initial part of the process of possible purchase.

The first stage in such a transaction is normally that the selling company, usually with the advice of an investment or merchant bank, makes available a limited amount of information about the company which is for sale. It is normal to ask for, and to have signed, a confidentiality letter, so that in the event that one of the purchasers does not proceed, the information supplied on this confidential basis will not be used by existing or future competitors. Once this information is received, it is checked against the already existing information about the target company. Very often the information which is provided serves only to corroborate, to a large extent, the information which was already available. However, any discrepancies are highlighted and keen attempts made to reach a reconciliation between the new information and the information which was previously held.

A number of internal functions in the company would be involved at this stage. The acquisitions team acts as coordinator for the activity, working closely with the business or businesses which have responsibility for the product range of the target company. Finance, legal, strategic planning and personnel departments would normally be involved at this initial stage in order to begin forming views and opinions about their respective areas of the target company.

On the basis of this activity and this new information, an updated review is produced. The next stage in the auction process is usually a request to submit an indicative, financial value which one would be prepared to pay for the target company. This is normally at this first stage not legally binding and is used by the seller to draw up a shortlist of companies to proceed with in an attempt to secure an eventual sale. The updated review would be presented to the ICI Board which would then decide whether or not to give authority to move on to the next stage, i.e. to indicate a probable value for the company. Once again, at this stage, any potential problem areas would be highlighted and might be stated by the Board to be conditions which need to be satisfied before a final bid could be made.

The seller then reviews the bids which have been submitted and decides with which companies or company he will proceed. At this stage he will normally offer further detailed information about the company and the possibility of discussions with management and visits to the facilities.

Upon receipt of the go-ahead that the company has been selected to participate in the final stage, ICI would move into the third, final and detailed stage. A group of people, varying in size depending upon the value and complexity of the transaction, would be allocated on a full-time basis to carry out the process which is known in the United States as 'due diligence'.

Due diligence procedures

The importance and value of professional due diligence in a transaction of this nature cannot be overstated. The selling company has a responsibility to present facts honestly about the company. However, it is not obliged to describe every detail or to highlight every potential problem. An example of what the selling company is obliged to do and equally what it is not permitted to do can be made by analogy to a transaction we are all familiar with: the purchase of a house. When describing the particulars of a house, the measurements of the rooms, the type of facilities, etc. all have to be itemised correctly. Any wise prospective purchaser will have some kind of professional survey to examine any major faults which should be apparent. However, it is not the responsibility of the vendor to make decisions on when new maintenance will be required, whether the house can or cannot be extended, how the value of the house might change, etc. These are the decisions which the purchaser has to make on the basis of whatever information he can find out.

In ICI a comprehensive due diligence manual is drawn up at this stage. An attempt is made to list all potential questions which should be asked about this company. (See Appendix B for a typical due diligence paper. Although this example is geared to a US acquisition, and some of the nomenclature may be unfamiliar in the UK, the areas which need to be covered are comprehensively defined and described and should prove useful to all transactions.)

Apart from obvious questions, such as sales value, financial figures, commercial status, etc., other equally important areas relate to research and development, engineering, pensions, insurance, terms and conditions of employment, and a multitude of other topics.

It is highly unlikely in any transaction that all these questions will be answered. However, it is important that the list of questions is comprehensive. It is equally unlikely that any prospective vendor will answer each question line by line, or frame the answer in the context in which the question has been posed. The process of due diligence is very much like peeling an onion. It has to be done layer by layer and at times can make one cry!

If the acquisition is a particularly large one – say, several billions of pounds – the personnel involved in the due diligence activity will need to be large and structured into teams. In the case of the largest transaction made by ICI, the purchase of Stauffer Chemical Company, approximately 125 people were involved at the peak of the due diligence process. It is clearly not possible for 125 people to meet and discuss the progress of due diligence. A hierarchy of teams was therefore developed which led to what became known as the core team which served to pull together, correlate and question all the information which had been received.

At this stage, if not earlier, it is useful to bring in relevant external experts. These may be investment bankers, who are able to do external valuations for comparison with the internal valuations which have been made. Alternatively, they may be experts in particular fields, for example, if there is a problem in the pensions area, it might be useful to bring in external pensions experts in order to get the best possible view.

The end of the due diligence is always unsatisfactory from the point of view of the prospective purchaser. As more and more becomes known about the company, more and more questions are raised. As the level of detail increases, the nature of the questions becomes more detailed and hence more difficult to answer. In the end there will always be a number of unanswered questions and a judgement will have to be made on the risk factor of these unanswered questions.

Decision day

Finally in ICI comes decision day. A final presentation is made to the Board asking for authority to try to conclude the transaction. At this stage everything is displayed – not just financial evaluations, but worries, concerns, problems and potential solutions. The important area of post-acquisition management is also addressed. It is important to know before making the final offer how the new company will be structured and incorporated in the existing company if the offer is successful. Too many companies make the mistake of concentrating on the acquisition and not worrying about post-acquisition management until after the company has been acquired. This can be a painful, and at times a fatal, mistake.

Once formal approval is given to a particular price and any conditions specifically laid out, the final, formal offer is made. This is submitted in writing, normally in accordance with a previously decided deadline. The final bids are examined and a decision made by the selling company which company to select.

However, it is very often not the end of the process. Quite often a number of bids are quite similar, and even if they are not, sometimes selling companies claim that they are, in order to have a final opportunity to maximise the value which they obtain for the company. In any event, the offer normally contains more than just a price figure. There will be some conditions, perhaps relating to verification of indebtedness or matters of that type. At least one more meeting is usually necessary in order to clarify exactly what is meant by the written words submitted before an offer is accepted.

If the offer is successful the final phase is then entered of contract preparation and signing. This can be a long and involved stage and a very important one since it is during this process that the final details of liabilities and warranties and issues of this type are resolved.

It may seem that little has been said about negotiations in the last few pages. Nothing could be further from the truth. Every aspect of this process contains negotiations determining the amount of information which will be made available during the various stages of due diligence; establishing the level of detail in which financial data, in particular, will be presented; determining the rules for conversation with management; and agreeing the number, length and duration of visits to facilities. All have to be negotiated. Similarly, the final stage between written offer and final acceptance can be a very intense and important negotiation. When transactions involving several million pounds are involved a 1 or 2 per cent difference becomes very significant.

Referring back to due diligence, it often happens that when a large company is bought some parts of it will be divested, because they are not relevant to the purchaser's company. By the same token, this means that the acquiring company knows less about these particular activities than about the part of the company which it is retaining. It is therefore doubly important, albeit doubly difficult, to carry out comprehensive due diligence on these parts of the company. There have been a number of examples in the press where failure to concentrate properly on the parts of the acquired company to be divested have turned what has apparently looked like a good deal into a highly expensive one for the acquiring company.

Finally, one golden rule. At each stage in the process check and re-check the information and the objective. It is easy in moving into more and more detailed analysis of a company to forget the main objective of the potential purchase. A check on whether or not in the final analysis the strategic objective will be achieved by this purchase, rather than whether or not it is simply a good bargain, is imperative.

Negotiating the deal

DAVID MICHAELS
Chairman, Guidehouse Group

Introduction

Negotiation is both an art and a science. You can develop the finesse of the art by experience, observation and inspiration but first it is helpful to assimilate and learn some of the techniques of the science. Negotiation affects every aspect of life and many of the techniques developed in the course of day-to-day living have been acquired by intuition and the self-discovery of methodology that either works or doesn't work in individual cases. The purpose of this chapter is to help you build upon your own techniques and then apply them to the negotiations involved in the purchase or sale of a business.

Everyday matters, such as negotiating a salary rise, obtaining a better room in a hotel, or a parking place at the office, through to the acceptance of a marriage proposal or success in a major job application all require the setting of an objective and a target. The mind quickly works out an effective route towards meeting the target by setting the scene, laying traps or 'bonuses' to be picked up later at a tactical point in time, combined with dogged persistence in meeting the objective.

More weighty political matters, such as the negotiation of the return of occupied territory, or the obtaining of significant concessions at superpower summits require very detailed definition of the target and the complicated route to reaching it. A summary of alternative concessions that might be made en route if needed, and a minimum and maximum position on each topic, is carefully and formally defined by each negotiating team in their private preparations. The definition of the agenda, where the meetings are to be held, and who should speak first, are all major tactical activities and each skirmish successfully won can be an important aspect and building-block towards creating success in meeting the ultimate objective.

By contrast, buying and selling a company is no more than a subset of such multidimensional international political negotiations. It is, however, more complicated than the simple bartering when buying or selling a secondhand car. Although the end product is primarily the definition of the subject of the offer and then its purchase for a satisfactory price, these ends are often best obtained by similar techniques to those applied in all negotiations for effectively setting the right atmosphere and negotiation process.

Some of the key characteristics of this process will be reviewed first in this chapter. The next logical step is to look at aspects of price formulation, packaging and agreement. It will then be useful to put all this into perspective by touching on several of the basic strategies for creating negotiation situations and for countering problems. Lastly, there is a review of the most important topic pervading the whole negotiation process – the completion of a transaction. This should not be seen as a separate subject but more as the culmination of the total negotiation process. Effectively using a range of techniques can improve the chances of success significantly, based upon a given endowment of comparative negotiating strength. The examples in this chapter relate primarily to the negotiations for the purchase of a private company and can be considered either from the point of view of the buyer or of the seller.

The negotiating process

At every stage, from conception to completion, a continuing analysis of the psychology and identity of the two sides, and of their aims and objectives, will identify essential pointers to effectively achieving an optimum negotiation.

Inception

It is often the case that, at the initial stages, objectives are not formulated in any precise financial terms on either side. The purchaser has the general notion that the business ought to be bought as cheaply as possible and on the best terms, and the vendor wants to sell it on as favourable terms as possible. It is obviously important but often neglected to decide and define clearly and at an early stage what is being bought in financial and commercial terms, and also to consider and take advice on the feasibility and probability of a successful outcome on both the worst and on the best price and commercial expectations which are likely to arise in the discussions ahead. This basic objective setting is often relegated to a far later point in the negotiation. Matters raised early and agreed in principle are very hard to change later and may become immutable and valuable points of principle not open for further discussions by the other side. Therefore, from whichever point of view you are coming, it is very helpful to establish these points at a very early stage.

Status of the parties

It is valuable to assess at an early stage both the real and the apparent comparative strengths of the two proponents from the financial, commercial and other points of view. This review should take into account the respective sizes and parameters of the balance sheet, the market capitalisation, market positions of the companies, and the reputation and renown of the personalities involved. Such a review might be intimidating for a company negotiating with GEC – unless you are as big as Hanson Trust. It is therefore valuable from whatever point of view to improve your apparent and perceived status. Means of achieving this include forging strong alliances, obtaining very good PR, appointing a major merchant bank to undertake the negotiations, arranging meetings in prestige offices, and so on. There are obvious dangers in creating 'puff' for its own sake but clearly the other party must give maximum credence to your statements and undertakings and have suitable concern about breaching confidences or undertakings given to or by you.

At an early stage it is important to establish the ability of the parties to commit their side. Are you negotiating with the principal, i.e. someone able immediately to make a decision, or are you negotiating with someone who must consult with head office? It is important to try to negotiate with the decision-maker. However, for your part it may well be useful to hide behind a mandate, e.g. 'I cannot recommend that to my shareholders', or 'I will see what my board makes of your offer', or 'my boss will only agree to a 5 per cent discount'. It is often easier to be aggressive with the other side if you are not the principal ('It's not me who disagrees but I cannot make any compromise or concession without referring back'). In the case of a quoted vendor, the position is often unclear anyway. The directors in a bid situation may ostensibly be acting for shareholders to get the best price but it is reasonable to expect that they would have in mind optimising their own positions at the same time.

Both sides enter negotiations with different strengths in terms of cash resources, ability and requirement to do a deal, market position, sanctions if the deal does not proceed, and so on. As we saw earlier, it is an important objective to improve perceived status. This will help get an early and easy concession to your point of view or requirement. When it comes to considering the position of advisers, there may well be all sorts of conflicts confusing the negotiation process. Does the adviser also lend money to the company or own shares in it? How will they feel about losing a client if that client is taken over? Are they business brokers working purely on a success-related basis, or will they receive a fee whatever the outcome? Will they get a higher fee on a successful transaction for the same time involvement, and so on? It is important to review the difficult and delicate balance between impartiality and motivation of advisers whether they are acting for a seller or a buyer. Sometimes advisers are appointed specifically to give independent advice. But the use of advisers can be important as a negotiating tool: 'My advisers will not let me take such a low offer!' Or, 'although my client wishes to deal on those terms, I cannot advise him to do so.'

The first meetings

One way of improving the negotiating strength of your side is to set the environment for the first meetings to enhance your particular case. You are not expected to go as far as world class chess masters who often deliberately create a stressful environment prior to and during a game in order to undermine the opponent! But you should consider the following questions:

1. Where should the first meetings be?
2. Who should be the host?
3. How should the meetings be conducted?
4. Should you put the parties in your boardroom with a rectangular table, or should all the parties meet around a circular table at a lunch or dinner?
5. Should the vendor let the buyer make the running in order to give the impression of being a reluctant seller?

Often these matters are ignored and discussions get off to a bad start quite unnecessarily.

At the early meetings it is useful to agree the broad parameters of the topics to be covered and negotiated upon, e.g. the initial payment, acceptability of deferred payments and period of time, service contracts, scope of investigations by the buyer, expectations of warranties and indemnities, etc. It is sometimes helpful to establish in advance procedures to cover disagreements between the parties. Sometimes it is important to document and minute the various meetings, and at other times it is helpful to leave matters undecided if you cannot get your own way initially.

Reading and controlling the situation

One should always listen carefully at meetings and look for the hidden signs. Is that 'no' really a 'perhaps'? At meetings people make non-verbal yes's and no's. Think about whether to hold short or long meetings –

some professionals work on through the night to settle a transaction on the basis that the other side might well reveal their hand when tired, or may compromise in order to bring these exhausting meetings to a close.

It is valuable in setting the scene to get easy and early agreement to non-contentious issues. Above all it is useful to focus on the issues in hand rather than personalities. If you are faced with an awkward character who is advising the vendor of a business you are trying to buy, ignore him; he and his client both probably think he is just doing his job.

Try not to say 'no' or 'never' in response to an offer or a question. It is often possible to answer 'yes' or 'possibly' to disarm the other party and then counter and continue with your own interpretation of the point in hand.

The negotiation process

All negotiations proceed from initial meetings through to more detailed meetings and visits. It is often useful to get to a heads of agreement early which schedules systematically all the points under negotiation. The most expedient negotiations I have seen move rapidly to documentation of all points of agreement and disagreement and from there to draft contracts. Specific meetings are then held by the principals on matters of disagreement. If these cannot be solved easily, the advisers then meet separately to seek technical solutions which go some way towards meeting each side's objectives. If it is essential or at least expedient to obtain an early transaction, it is sometimes helpful to have both sides sign a definitive but conditional contract which schedules a number of open conditions precedent, e.g. a satisfactory accountants' investigation, verification of asset levels, the entering of service agreement, the availability of finance, and so on. It may then be possible for both sides to move to solve the open questions without reopening the other contracted matters which have been agreed.

Above all remember that the object of the negotiations is to come to a successful completion and therefore do focus on essentials. Decide whether a particular matter is a point of principle or merely a detail – the perception of the two parties may well be different on such matters. From start to finish, the negotiation process should be harmonious, target (i.e. completion)-driven, and fundamentally should define clearly at an early stage the decisions that are required to be made and the documents that are required to be settled. Meetings should resolve open questions systematically without, if possible, opening previously agreed areas and climaxing in the completion.

The actual negotiation process should also foreshadow the post-acquisition management. Buying the company is no more than 'winning

the war'! It is 'winning the peace', i.e. the later successful management
and integration, that is so important to the buyer. It is probably equally
important to the seller if there is some type of deferred payment regime
or if the long-term future after integration within the buying organisation
is valued.

Price parameters and techniques

We have reviewed the background and foreshadowed the foreground in
the negotiation process. Now it is time to start talking about the price.
What are the groundrules? Like tennis, it is often how you hit that
determines how you may receive a reply. Most negotiating positions are
put to best advantage, based upon the effective use of technical points and
detailed contents rather than relying on personality and intuition. Many
people enter negotiations with the confidence that they can obtain a strong
'feel' from the way the price discussion goes as to what the vendor will
accept for the company or what the buyer will pay.

It is important, however, to prepare the valuation carefully as soon
as the financial parameters are available. In coming to the valuation it is
necessary to do an *overall* audit of the position. This chapter is not the place
to review in detail methods of valuation but it is useful to schedule amongst
other matters the profit history, profit projection, asset values, market
position, management strength, management remuneration expectations,
tax position, and so on (see Chapter 3). A review of valuations of
quoted companies and the sale of similar unquoted companies can help
to gain a market perception of the open market price of the company in
question. Wherever possible it is useful to take the opportunity to define
parameters or to identify areas which will be useful for trade-offs in the
price negotiations which will follow later. It may well be true that the
to-and-fro banter of buyer and seller discussion *is* required to establish
the other side's parameters, but these parameters themselves may actually
be misguided. With detailed preparation it is often possible to obtain an
indication of the actual open market *value*. The buyer can change the
vendor's appraisal of the value; or the vendor can convince the purchaser
more effectively with facts, figures and statistics. Merely holding out
intuitively for a lower or higher price will often leave the other side
feeling dissatisfied: it is important for the other side to feel they have got
a good deal.

The buyer and seller should reflect on their minimum and maximum
price requirements before entering a face-to-face discussion. In the heat
of an auction, it is well known that a bidder will go well above his initial
price maximum if he has not learned the discipline of robustly defining a
price and keeping to it. The main technique of price negotiations depends

upon a broad assessment of the other side's minimum and maximum and getting them to believe that they have negotiated a price on your side which is their assessment of your minimum or maximum (as the case may be). In other words, they have to second-guess your limits and *also* have the feeling that they have negotiated you to your limit if they are to feel they have got a good or, at least, adequate deal. Your objective appears to be to communicate some parameters to the other side in such a way that they feel that they know your figures. These will not of course necessarily be your *true* limits!

Price strategy

On the question of who should make the first price play, there are times when it is helpful to be vague and obtain a feeling from the other side before making a commitment on your side. On balance, it is often best to open reasonably early with your own price within a range, since this sets the correct atmosphere for the price discussions within your limits rather than within those of the other side. If you state a price range, the other side will calculate the most favourable end of this range – extremes may be unacceptable to either side. If for example you will accept a price of £1 million for your business, you can set the expectations on the other side by saying that you have been advised that the business is worth between £1.25 and £1.5 million and that you will only accept a price in this range. Obviously every particular negotiation is different and depends significantly on the facts and figures of the case. However in this particular case it is difficult for a potential buyer prepared to pay £750,000–1,250,000 to open with an initial range of £500,000–750,000 since this would obviously fall upon deaf ears.

There are some pricing strategies which if used badly can sometimes rebound. An example is the 'highball'. This is a situation where a buyer makes an outrageously high initial offer in order to get a seller talking and eliminate all other bidders. The buyer then systematically negotiates his own offer price downward by highlighting a range of matters that in his view diminishes the price. A 'lowball' can be put in by a buyer to demoralise a seller and radically lower his expectations. Alternatively, a seller can use a 'lowball' to interest a buyer by saying that he will sell at a low price. The seller then raises the price steadily by reinterpreting the 'lowball' to augment that price by requiring payment for other aspects that the seller had not deemed to be included in that original price. A deal that originally seemed cheap and attractive and encouraged a buyer to enter serious discussions can therefore be talked up to more acceptable levels by the seller.

The next rule covers obtaining movement on the price on either side.

You shouldn't move until there has been a counter-offer of some type. Unilateral moves are wasteful. Never just concede a price – get something for it! All price movement should be made in small steps to establish by signs and pointers to the other side a minimum to maximum range in order to give the other side the impression that you have gone as far as you are prepared to go. If, in the above example, you get an offer of £900,000 refer to your own original range and say that you would be prepared to accept the minimum (i.e. £1 million) or perhaps £5,000 or £10,000 below it. Small movements of price around your target figure will maintain the integrity of the target. In particular never 'split the difference' between two prices. Get a *quid pro quo* for agreeing to split the difference, e.g. ask the other side to pay the legal fees or to defer part of the price for, say, one year as a consideration of splitting.

Packaging

In the earlier, preparation, stage it was suggested that you should identify those areas which may be suitable for trade-off in the price negotiation. You should review these in some depth using lateral thinking to try to create a package that is in effect bigger for both of you. It is not so much a question of arguing about dividing the pie between you but of appearing to make it larger from both points of view. It is possible to package the price and make it more attractive by suggesting an element of deferment. Payment can be made in cash, shares, loan stock, and so on. Commercial benefits can be added which are sometimes considered more valuable than the cash equivalent alone, e.g. corporate status, holidays, motor cars, and so on. It may even be worth offering to pay legal and accounting fees. Broadly, the pricing strategy is a matter of determining the overall valuation requirement for both sides in which the price is just one of the parameters – £5 million over five years is not as valuable as £5 million today, but packaging the deal in this way might be the only method of finding an acceptable compromise for both sides. In the pricing discussions it helps if you keep the parameters moving and when you can see the shape of a package that appeals to you then tighten up on each parameter, trading acceptable points for those that are unacceptable. As stated before, both sides should feel they have stretched each other to their maximum or minimum respective positions.

Strategies

All deals progress through various stages which either evolve or are shaped by deliberate design on either side. Sometimes a negotiation strategy seems to emerge; at other times both sides agree to take a particular route in order to meet their mutual objectives. The negotiating teams can design to change the strategy perceptibly or imperceptibly to achieve advantage. But what are these strategies? Some form part of wider game plans and can be merged as the negotiations progress. However, they usually have some fairly basic components or identities.

Basic strategy

It is recognised that to obtain a satisfactory deal and make the other side believe that what has been achieved is worthwhile you have to haggle. Even if the price is acceptable immediately a buyer and seller should feel that they have won a good deal from the other side by having had to work to achieve it. How many times have you felt that you have offered or accepted too much or too little in an individual negotiation? It is also useful to *tell* the other side that they have got a good deal. They can then have the satisfaction of knowing this.

Tough approach

This is usually a relatively successful approach between parties of unequal status. It is a situation epitomised by 'Unless you sell me the company for £1 million I will cancel your franchise for our product forthwith!' It is a 'sign here or else' situation and involves setting deadlines and bringing in competitive buyers or sellers. This strategy relies on the strength of the respective negotiating positions since it is hard to achieve success under such pressure between equal-status parties. Sometimes it is valuable to recognise or anticipate early if someone is going to take this tough approach and to pre-empt the situation by a similar or complementary position. If you then receive a deadline or ultimatum you 'see the bluff' by accepting, subject to your own stringent conditions. Normally it is not possible to respond in kind. You cannot fight a sumitomo wrestler at his own sport but it only required a stone to fell Goliath who thought he was fighting with swords.

Good guy/bad guy

This approach is often useful for 'allowing' the counter-party to gauge your maximum and minimum limits. It allows you to communicate through a dialogue with an executive from your own side your apparent thinking – e.g. 'Look, John, you know the Board have only authorised us to go up to £1 million.' 'Well then I will take it upon my own shoulders to go up to £1.1 million and that will be our maximum', and so on. This approach is often useful for allowing and obtaining minor concessions, particularly if they can encompass all outstanding points and lead to an early completion.

Referring back

It is sometimes very useful to make it clear right from the beginning of a negotiation that you personally cannot make a decision without your adviser or without the agreement of others. It may be in some cases that you can only speak for 40, 50 or 60 per cent and you therefore need the other side's help in presenting the case in the best light to the shareholders. It is easier to be contrary and tough face-to-face with a counter-party if you are not the principal but are merely expressing their views or your instructions, e.g. 'I do not think I can remotely get my shareholders to agree to make such a high bid for your company' or 'I am sure my old grandmother and the trustees would not accept such a low offer!' You therefore negotiate with the other side to the best of your ability a set of parameters which you take back to the negotiating table later to obtain further concessions if possible.

Immovable mountain

Sometimes one recognises when the counter-party has dug in their heels, either in private or in public, and therefore cannot withdraw from a stated position, e.g. 'We would not accept less than £1 per share under any circumstance!' Here it is important to persuade the principal not to take an entrenched position and to help in representing to the other side reasons why such a firm position should now be 'reinterpreted'. It is usually too high a risk taking such a closed position on your side since as a bluff tactic it may rebound upon you. You are more likely to see this position taken by the other side. But it is possible to present a variant of the ultimatum in a somewhat less aggressive format: 'I can see no particular reason why I should offer more than £2 per share and therefore that is where my best offer will remain until Friday unless you can persuade me otherwise with facts and figures.'

Deadlock

It is occasionally impossible to reconcile price and package differences. Even a shuffle backwards and forwards between the parties by advisers and intermediaries may be ineffective in these circumstances. It is important therefore to find other points of contact or reasons for doing the transaction; lateral thinking or creativity may be the only way of rescuing such a transaction. To present equality of sacrifice may be the only fair way of meeting both sides' aspirations. You or the other side could take an absolutely entrenched position as a technique for assessing the determination of the counter-party to conclude the transaction. As stated before, this stance can rebound and a deal can be lost. You should ascertain whether the other side is taking this position as a strategy or as an expression of an honestly held position.

Completion

It is useful here just to touch upon the object of the whole exercise – completion of the deal. The American term 'closing' is perhaps quite apt. Techniques for achieving this successfully are very important. From an early stage get agreement on a target completion date. Refer to it constantly and get the bankers, lawyers and advisers all committed to working towards this date. It is useful to prepare and agree a timetable of key landmarks towards such a completion. Long-drawn-out deals often fall apart for lack of momentum. Once a basic agreement is reached on the main issues, the momentum should be increased to document and conclude the transaction.

It is useful to plan meetings well in advance as a series rather than from one to the next. Increase the frequency of the scheduled meetings in the period leading up to completion. In the final period it is useful to have two levels of meeting, to cover points of principle, and to cover technical details. Have a rehearsal completion meeting to finalise wherever possible all the key issues. This should also identify those few remaining sticking points. If attitudes are well attuned towards completion at an early stage and all parties synchronise their social and business diaries accordingly, then a satisfactory schedule can be adhered to. In the end it may well be helpful for the parties to arrange in advance an all-day/night meeting to finalise the paperwork. If it is seen that the completion itself is part of the negotiation process, the resolution of outstanding issues can be facilitated. For example, if there are still imponderables left open at a late stage, be prepared to have the parties sign a binding agreement subject to the various conditions outstanding.

Principals should always meet socially for both general discussions and reviews about the business outside of the main negotiating meeting. They should have the opportunity to talk about the business in an environment where price and other parameters are not being hammered out. This will help develop a strong business relationship and mutual commitment in their combined interests in the completion of the transaction. It is helpful if they recognise and communicate to their advisers that it is the principals who are the main losers if the deal comes unstuck; the advisers often merely get slightly lower fees if the deal aborts. As a technique it is useful to save a

minor compromise to assist the final settlement of all outstanding points
of a deal on the basis of a *quick* completion, e.g. 'we will agree to pay the
fees of all parties if we can complete by tomorrow night.'

Conclusion

It is hoped that the reader will identify an integrated approach to
the whole negotiation process with a predetermined strategy through to
completion to maximise the chances of the successful deal. We have noted
that personal qualities are important in setting the atmosphere throughout
the negotiation process: humour and a positive attitude between the parties
can overcome some of the worst problems.

As regards the crucial aspect of price, and the packaging of the price,
both sides must feel that they have achieved a larger slice in a larger pie.
This should be packaged and presented to take account of each side's
aspirations and to accommodate commercial reality. Detailed research
pays off handsomely, particularly on the side of the vendor. The parties
should not rely solely on their negotiating ability and *nous* to assess the
best price they can achieve. They might achieve the best price but it might
also be the wrong one!

Although transactions have their natural momentum they also have
their moments of inertia, therefore energy, design and careful scheduling
are needed to push a transaction towards a successful conclusion. Much
work can be wasted by a deal failing at the last hurdle for lack of
agreement on minor points. The principals should develop a method
of communication with each other which is rehearsed and prepared
at an early stage in order to avoid these last-minute collapses. It goes
without saying that it is easy to repent at leisure if the acquisition
has been ill-conceived; but in emphasising the completion process, it is
considered that the parties wish to proceed with the transaction and that
the post-acquisition management has been planned adequately.

Finally don't tell anyone else the various secrets that have been imparted
to you as you may meet them on the other side of the negotiation table.
Don't be afraid or intimidated by a skilful negotiator on the other side.
Such a confrontation can often circumvent a long series of negotiations
and it can be a welcome relief in dealing with a professional. In the end,
reversion to a simple and open declaration of your position and relying
upon intuition may indeed be the most satisfactory way to cut out the
posturing and reach a successful and profitable conclusion. After all you
can always say No!

Chapter 6

Legal aspects of acquisitions

IAN F. ELDER

Solicitor

Scope

This chapter is written principally on the assumption that the target company is a limited liability company incorporated in the United Kingdom, although much of the material will be relevant to acquisitions elsewhere. Some introductory remarks on the legal status of the target and the seller may be helpful.

Legal status of the target

The simplest form of business organisation is the sole trader, whose business assets and liabilities are in general not distinguishable for legal purposes from the owner's personal assets and liabilities. The liability of members of a partnership is also usually unlimited. (Limited partnerships do exist but they are used for special reasons and are not a common form of business organisation.) Most non-communist economies recognise the concept of a limited liability company as a means of business organisation. Unlike a sole trader or partnership, a limited liability company is a legal person, distinct from its shareholders and with its own rights and obligations. Each shareholder's obligation is limited to paying-up the full amount on his shares in the company. Having done so, he cannot be called upon to contribute more, irrespective of the liabilities incurred by the company (except in special circumstances, notably where fraud is established).

The vast majority of acquisitions in the UK are of limited liability companies, as opposed to businesses conducted by sole traders or partnerships, and the same is likely to be true in the other non-communist economies. However, for tax and other reasons a purchaser may be faced with, or may benefit from, buying a business rather than a company's shares and the main differences are considered later in this chapter.

Legal status of the seller

Whether it is a business or a company that is being acquired, the legal status of the seller is important. This is not only to ensure that the seller has sufficient legal power and authority to make the sale and to transfer legal title to the buyer, but also to ensure that (creditworthiness apart) remedies for breach of contact can be enforced by the buyer.

The seller will often itself be a limited liability company, in which case the same principles of limited liability (considered briefly above) apply to it as much as to the target. Moreover, the principle of limited liability is generally applicable to each company within a group, i.e. if the seller is a subsidiary company its holding company will not be liable beyond the paid-up capital in the subsidiary. It is prudent therefore to ensure that if the seller is not the parent company, and is not a company of substance in its own right, any obligations are assumed directly by, or are guaranteed by, the parent company of the group.

The seller may, of course, be an individual or collection of individuals, a partnership, a trustee, an administrator, a receiver or a liquidator – each situation will involve different considerations for the buyer and his advisers.

Purchase of a business

If all the shares of a company are being acquired, it follows that all the assets and liabilities of the target company will fall under the purchaser's control. (In this chapter it is assumed that 100 per cent control is acquired; acquisitions of less than 100 per cent require special consideration.)

If however only a 'business' is being acquired, only those assets and liabilities used in the business will be acquired. This can be advantageous to both seller and buyer in certain circumstances. One of the most attractive aspects from the buyer's point of view is that identified assets and liabilities can be acquired which do not involve the same risk of undisclosed liabilities, as is the case in the acquisition of a company. In general, liabilities do not pass to the buyer of a business, although contracts of employment of employees in European Economic Community (EEC) countries are now transferred by operation of law to purchasers of businesses within the EEC.

Equally, however, contracts in the name of the seller have to be assigned to and assumed by the purchaser, which often requires the consent of third parties; this is rarely necessary in the case of the sale of the shares of a company as the identity of the company does not change. The necessity to obtain these consents often provides third parties with a lever to renegotiate unprofitable contracts or to exact some other price for their consent. Moreover, certain benefits, e.g. accrued tax losses, cannot be transferred to the purchaser of a business, whereas they may remain available if the shares of the company (which has the benefit of the tax loss) are purchased.

Jurisdictions

Acquisitions are complicated if any one of the seller, the buyer or the target company/business is located in a different legal jurisdiction. The seller is of course primarily concerned with obtaining payment and will often have little further concern once the price is received. However, in certain instances, the price may be payable in instalments (perhaps by reference to future performance of the target or as a surety for non-breach of warranty by the seller) in which case there will be concern about the buyer's future ability to make payment. The buyer may be resident in one jurisdiction, be buying in a different legal jurisdiction and may have to enforce rights against the seller in a third.

Local legal advice is essential in all relevant legal jurisdictions and can affect not only the contents of the documentation but often the structure of the transaction. Obtaining this advice, even in general terms, should therefore be undertaken at an early stage.

Competition and other regulatory approvals

'Public policy' considerations limit the free acquisition of companies and businesses in a variety of jurisdictions by imposing so-called 'merger controls'. ('Merger' in this context does not necessarily denote the coming together of parties of equal size; it is so defined as to include acquisitions of companies and businesses which meet the relevant criteria.) Restrictions are commonly imposed to prevent the creation or enhancement of monopolies but they are often supported by wider considerations of 'public policy' which can, for instance, restrict the acquisition of domestic concerns by 'foreigners'. This 'foreign' acquisition need not be judged even by national boundaries; regional interests may also fall to be protected in the public interest.

The approval of the appropriate authorities is usually a precondition to any acquisition. Such approval may be mandatory, as under the US Hart–Scott–Rodino Antitrust Improvements Act, or may simply be prudent. In the United Kingdom there is no mandatory approval, but if a merger is the subject of an adverse report by the Monopolies and Mergers Commission, the acquirer can be forced to divest the whole or a part of the target. The risk of this is usually so serious that the acquirer will be

advised to make it a precondition that clearance or comfort is obtained
before he makes an unconditional commitment.

While hitherto the EEC Commission has not enjoyed any formal
power to control mergers of companies, it is likely that it will soon have
specific merger controls which will be additional to the merger controls
exercised in the various Member States. The relationship between the
EEC and Member State controls is currently the subject of much heated
debate.

Heads of Agreement/Letters of Intent

'Heads of Agreement' or 'Letters of Intent' are often used by the parties
to establish the major principles of the agreement before formal
agreements are entered into. In English legal terminology they are generally
understandings which are 'subject to contract', i.e. they are not intended
by the parties to be legally binding in themselves but are subject to the
conclusion of fully negotiated contracts. They are generally loathed by
lawyers and much favoured by their business clients!

The negotiations for the acquisition of companies or businesses can
often take months or even years before the buyer and seller agree the basic
terms, in particular the price. Someone in business, understandably, does
not wish to be dogged by a lawyer at each twist and turn of this process.
Having 'done the deal' he wishes to evidence it in some joint document,
often so that he can proceed with some confidence to obtain the support
of colleagues or superiors.

The lawyer is concerned that by signing a piece of paper (which the
lawyer often has not seen) his client is committed to the acquisition,
at worst legally and at best morally, without realising the full
implications.

There is no easy answer to this dilemma. It is clearly important for the
parties to be sure that the basic 'deal' is there before they proceed to the
upheaval and expense involved in setting the acquisition in train. Equally
however, an ill-considered Letter of Intent can severely restrict flexibility
while the negotiation of a fully-termed one can consume valuable time
which is better spent in progressing the legally binding agreement.

Advisers

Both the buyer and the seller need to involve their advisers at the
earliest date that a deal is imminent. If the buyer is bringing in a
merchant/investment banker, he will usually know when to involve
other professional advisers. Lawyers, accountants, brokers, tax, pension,

personnel and publicity advisers may all be needed. Pension and personnel advisers will usually be necessary where any substantial body of employees is involved and early regard to employee considerations is usually vital in the success of any such acquisition.

Quoted and unquoted companies

There is usually a marked difference between the acquisition of shares of companies which are quoted on a Stock Exchange in the country in question (i.e. those held by 'the public') and those which are held by a few private individuals or a company within a group.

In the UK the terms 'private' and 'public' companies do not distinguish quoted companies and non-quoted companies; in order to be quoted a company must be a 'public' company but not all public companies are quoted. In this chapter however for convenience the term 'private company' is (unless otherwise indicated) used to mean a company which is not quoted, and 'public company' is used to mean a company quoted on a Stock Exchange. The vast majority of companies are private companies and their acquisition and disposal greatly exceed the acquisition and disposal of shares in public companies.

Any one of the target, the seller or the buyer may be a public company. The acquisition of public companies is usually subject to detailed regulation designed to protect the public against abuse, in particular by providing them with sufficient, independently verified, information on which to base a decision on whether to sell their shares. The same is true, although to a lesser extent, when the public are shareholders in the buyer or seller, because their approval of the management's decision to make a substantial acquisition or divestment may be necessary. The rules usually contain detailed provisions preventing market manipulation of quoted shares and ensuring equality of treatment of shareholders.

'Unfriendly' or 'hostile' takeovers are generally only possible where the shares are publicly held because only then can they be purchased in the market against the recommendation of the target's management. In private companies the directors are often substantial shareholders with an identity of interest as director, employee and shareholder. In public companies potential conflicts come to the fore when the directors are faced with an offer from a potential acquirer. Such an offer will usually have considerable implications for the directors personally which they must set aside in discharging their wider responsibilities. Independent advice is vital in this process.

Hostile takeovers still represent an extremely small proportion of acquisitions and while they give rise to strong emotions by the opponents of the free market on the one side and the advocates of 'public interest' concerns on the other, they remain a relatively expensive and harrowing form of purchase for all concerned. Most businesspeople will be fortunate in never being involved in the process although some specialists in hostile takeovers have proved that they can be a profitable method of breaking up inefficient conglomerates, which they also argue is a useful function of the market.

There is no doubt but that the existence and recent increase in hostile takeovers have caused management to have greater regard to their performance in their shareholders' eyes than hitherto. Dissatisfied shareholders' only other remedy is to enforce the removal of the Board of Directors of the company, which is seldom done in public companies or, at least, is seldom done openly.

In the UK, companies quoted on The International Stock Exchange in London are subject to the Rules governing the Admission of Securities to Listing (the 'Yellow Book') and acquisitions of quoted and unquoted public companies are subject to the City Code on Takeovers and Mergers (the 'Takeover Code') and the rules governing Substantial Acquisitions of Shares (SARs). (Offers for private companies may in certain circumstances also fall within the Takeover Code.) The Yellow Book is administered by the Council of the Stock Exchange; the Takeover Code and SARs by the Panel on Takeovers and Mergers. In addition to these rules are the statutory requirements, the most important of which is the Companies Act 1985, which regulates both private and public companies.

The General Principles which lie at the heart of the Takeover Code are reproduced at Appendix C. Although they generally only govern acquisitions of quoted and unquoted public companies they do represent a general statement of good practice in relation to the fair treatment of shareholders.

The price

The most important aspect of the agreement as between the seller and buyer is likely to be the price agreed for the purchase and sale of the shares or the business. (Lawyers call this the 'consideration' paid for what is being acquired.)

The price will usually be a payment in cash and may be payable as one single payment or in instalments. Clearly, if the seller has given assurances with respect to the company or the business, the buyer will be in a much stronger position to enforce any rights if part of the price is retained. If a retention is to be negotiated, however, the buyer should make it a fundamental condition of the agreement from the outset.

It is not unusual for the parties to agree to relate a part of the consideration to the performance of the company or business being acquired. These so called 'earn-outs' are superficially appealing to the buyer as they are only paid if the assets acquired are performing up to or above expectations. The difficulty which 'earn-outs' give rise to, however, is that they are extremely difficult to monitor unless the status quo in the business is maintained throughout the agreed period after the acquisition. This may be the buyer's intention at the time of the purchase but often, after entering the company, changes may be necessary. Any flexibility can be severely restricted by the existence of the 'earn-out'. Moreover, changes in customers and suppliers are a fact of business life and it is often not easy to single out a reason for any particular change. Recriminations will follow if the seller feels the buyer is altering the shape of the business to frustrate the 'earn-out', or if the buyer feels there are impediments in effectively managing the business by restrictions imposed to protect the seller's interests.

If an 'earn-out' is part of the business deal then the buyer is well advised to find a method of capping the maximum sum payable so that, if only as a last resort, it can be bought out in the event of the business needing to be fundamentally restructured or perhaps even sold on. The level of the 'cap' will be difficult to agree (the seller's scenario for business expansion will be lyrical at this point in the negotiations) and beware of fiscal and regulatory traps. Authorities faced with a formula of future performance will see the 'cap' as the only method of quantification and they are likely to levy tax or require approvals accordingly, however unrealistic in practice its achievement may be. Clearly the shorter the period of the earn-out the less the concern on having an agreed cap, and the converse applies.

The price need not be cash; it could be assets of some other kind or shares in the buyer. While the seller may be reluctant to accept shares in a private company because of their limited marketability, there may be a willingness to accept shares that are publicly traded, given sufficient safeguards as to their value at the time of issue. For the buyer it may be cheaper to raise the proceeds for the acquisition by issuing further shares. This can be done either directly to the seller or indirectly by arranging for the shares to be placed (sold in the market) for cash which can be used to pay the seller.

The Agreement

The seller knows what is being sold; the buyer (or buyer's advisers) know what protection a buyer is normally seeking. Who should draft the Acquisition Agreement?

Most practising lawyers would agree that the preparation of the agreement is an advantage and it is normally the prerogative of the buyer. If the time is available, the buyer is often well advised to prepare a list of enquiries (preliminary information), the responses to which can be used to tailor standard form agreements (and in particular warranties) for the particular transaction. (To avoid duplication this information should be used to form the basis of the Disclosure Letter, discussed below.)

A list of preliminary information in connection with an English private company acquisition is included by way of illustration at Appendix D.

The Agreement will usually cover all the mechanics of the acquisition including the calculation and payment of the price. The Agreement will be complicated if there is a delay between signature of the contract and Completion of the purchase (when the money is paid and shares/business transferred). This is because if the parties are committed at that point, subject only to external approvals, the question has to be faced of which party suffers if there is a deterioration in the business in the interim. Can the buyer rescind and/or claim damages? Can the seller compel the buyer to complete on the original terms even though the buyer has not been in control? There are no right answers to these questions; they have to be negotiated in the context of each particular transaction.

Unless there is a need for a delay between signature and completion however, e.g. because consents can only be obtained following signature, it is recommended that wherever possible all conditions are satisfied before signature, and completion takes place immediately after signature. This also means that the warranties and the Disclosure Letter (discussed below) can be given at Completion and not from an earlier signing date.

Warranties

The most time-consuming aspect of the legal negotiations for the acquisition of a private company (and to a lesser extent of a business) is usually in obtaining agreement on the terms of the Warranties and on the disclosures made with respect to them.

The purpose of the Warranties is to give the buyer reassurance from the seller as to the state of the company/business being acquired and to give legal force to the reliance placed on the 'facts' given which underpin the decision to make the acquisition. Most Acquisition Agreements will state that they supersede all earlier agreements or documents relating to the acquisition, so the buyer must ensure that all relevant data are expressly included as a warranty in the Acquisition Agreement.

In the US, the UK, Canada and Australia the practice of producing a schedule of warranties which runs to 30–40 closely typed pages is becoming common. Elsewhere in Western Europe the approach seems hitherto to have been more 'gentlemanly' but the signs are that the US practice will become the norm.

There is little point in setting out here the common warranties as styles can be found in specialist textbooks. However the following broad areas will usually be covered:

1. warranties that the seller can convey good title to the shares/business,
2. warranties that the target is properly constituted and has filed all necessary returns,
3. warranties that information provided is correct,
4. warranties as to the compliance by the target with all laws and regulations,
5. warranties that the target is not insolvent or on the verge of insolvency,
6. warranties that the target owns all the assets, licences and consents necessary to run its business, including all patents, trademarks, knowhow and (of increasing importance) computer systems,
7. warranties that there is no undisclosed pending or threatened litigation,
8. warranties that the target can stand alone, i.e. that there are no arrangements which will cease upon acquisition by the buyer which could distort the target's performance from that in the past,
9. warranties as to the accuracy of the last audited accounts and as to the performance of the target thereafter,
10. warranties as to the valuation of stock and fixed assets,
11. warranties as to the collectability of outstanding amounts receivable (book debts),
12. warranties that the target has not sold defective products,
13. warranties that all 'material' contracts have been disclosed,
14. warranties that all liabilities have been disclosed, including borrowings,
15. warranties as to the existence and adequacy of insurance cover,
16. warranties (which are usually extensive) as to the tax position of the target, in particular that it has paid or provided for all taxes which are due or accrued. (The cessation of the target from the seller's group can often have tax consequences for both the seller and the target.) Tax will usually be less of a concern where a business is being acquired as the liability to pay any tax will not normally be assumed by the buyer, although conversely, tax losses will not be available,
17. warranties as to the number and terms and conditions of employment of employees including (importantly) future pension entitlement and the adequacy of any relevant fund to meet existing and future claims.

This list is by no means exhaustive and particular facts and particular jurisdictions will require that new warranties be prepared and that standard form warranties be adapted.

Arguments about the scope of warranties can rage long into the night. To take an extreme but real example, suppose the buyer is

worried that the company being acquired may employ people who
have been exposed to harmful substances (e.g. asbestos) over the years
in the course of manufacturing the company's products. The usual form
of warranties would normally force disclosure before signature of any
known incidents, but what of latent injury? Suppose asbestosis has not yet
been diagnosed but is subsequently diagnosed after the acquisition. The
employees will seek compensation from the company which may or may
not be adequately insured to meet the claims. Frequently the warranties
will make the seller responsible for such matters, including those of which
he may not (and could not) have been aware, on the basis that the buyer
was entitled to make certain assumptions in agreeing the price. On the
other hand, when negotiating the warranties, the seller might well refuse
to accept even a proportionate liability for latent injury of this sort. There
is again no wrong or right answer; it is simply a matter of negotiation in
the circumstances.

The Disclosure Letter

It is convenient to deal with the Disclosure Letter here. The seller is usually
invited not to amend the warranties but rather to 'disclose' against them.
(In practice he usually does both to some extent.) The warranty is thus read
with the disclosure and only if the seller has failed to make a disclosure, or
has made an untrue disclosure, will he be liable for breach of warranty.
For instance, the warranty might say that the target had not created any
mortgages but the Disclosure Letter would identify that a mortgage had
been created on a particular day in favour of a particular lender, etc.
(This methodology is confusing to an inexperienced buyer or seller who
reads the first draft of the warranties and sees a number of statements
that all parties know are manifestly untrue. Resist the urge to 'correct'
the warranties!)

Inexperienced sellers will be advised, often against their initial instinct,
to disclose all that they possibly can because by doing so they limit their
liability for the warranties being given. The term 'Disclosure Letter' is
misleading in this respect because when it is taken together with the copy
documents and agreements it 'discloses', it can often extend to a bundle
of papers that would fill a drawer of a filing cabinet. Both the buyer
and his advisers have to read and digest these before signature to ensure
that there are no surprises in the disclosures and the warranties are not
qualified to an unacceptable degree.

Acquisitions of public companies do not generally include warranties
to anything like the same extent. The shares in public companies tend to
be so widely held that it is impractical to bind the selling shareholders to
the Acquisition Agreement in the same way as a seller of shares

in a private company. The more rigorous accounting and disclosure requirements required of public companies to maintain their quotation on Stock Exchanges, also usually afford a higher level of protection than is afforded in the case of a private company.

In a friendly takeover of a public company, i.e. one recommended for acceptance by the directors of the target, the buyer will at least have access to information about the target which may not be in the public domain. In a hostile takeover the buyer will not only not obtain warranties but will only have access to information which is publicly available.

Limitations on warranties

The seller will usually seek in the Acquisition Agreement to limit liability with respect to warranty claims by negotiating a maximum amount that can be required to be 'repaid' and by limiting the period within which claims must be notified. Fixing these limits is again a matter for negotiation in the context of the individual transaction.

A 2–3-year limit would probably be usual save with respect to tax claims which are usually permitted for the full period that the tax authority in the relevant jurisdiction can bring proceedings for recovery of the tax concerned.

The claim should only have to be *notified* within the period; it may well take months or years thereafter to assess and finally settle the liability.

As regards the financial limit, the parties often agree that the seller should not be required to repay more than the price and the limit is agreed at that level. There are examples however of unlimited liability for breach of warranty and equally limits have been set at a small percentage of the price. At the end of the day the negotiating strength of the parties in the particular transactions should determine the limits.

Indemnification

In the United Kingdom it is common in company acquisitions for a separate Deed of Indemnity to be entered into to which not only the buyer and seller are parties, but also the target and its subsidiaries. The Deed of Indemnity is generally confined to tax claims with respect to the period prior to the acquisition which may be more easily reimbursed by a payment from the seller to the target or subsidiary concerned than by calculating the buyer's 'loss' as a result of the unexpected tax charge.

The company's management

The directors (and indeed the employees generally) of the target are in a particularly difficult position during the acquisition process. Often only they have the detailed knowledge of the target necessary to make disclosures for the seller against the warranties. At the same time they know that their future will be bound up with the buyer if the acquisition is successful. While the seller would no doubt prefer them to give the warranties, if they did so the buyer would end up with a remedy against the management of its new subsidiary which would be highly unsatisfactory!

These conflicts are of course increased where the target company's management are themselves the purchaser of the business, as happens in management buy-outs. While many of the matters discussed above are equally applicable to such transactions, the financing and tax considerations are sufficiently specialised that they merit separate treatment outside the scope of this chapter.

Final thoughts

Businesspeople clearly do not want to involve a full team of professional advisers in negotiations before they know that an agreement in principle has been reached to sell and buy. However it is prudent before even a 'handshake' deal is made to consult with professional advisers on the general terms and outline structure of the transaction to ensure that significant issues are raised at a sufficiently early stage in negotiations. In practice, the handshake deal becomes the moral if not the legal reference point.

This is so to such an extent that buyers are generally extremely reluctant to seek a renegotiation of the price even where the 'disclosure exercise' results in the discovery of sizeable costs or liabilities of which the buyer was previously unaware. Whether this reluctance is a result of the momentum of the acquisition process, the inflexibility of management hierarchies, or the feeling that it is somehow 'ungentlemanly' to renegotiate the handshake deal is not clear, but it is a fact and it emphasises the importance of professional advice so that major issues can be identified and discussed before the agreement in principle is reached and the handshake deal done.

Chapter 7

Pensions and incentive arrangements

E. M. BELMONT

Divisional Director, Buck Paterson Consultants

Pensions
Introduction

Pensions are expensive. The assets of a company's pension scheme can easily exceed its annual wages bill. It is therefore essential when buying a company to understand the pension commitments involved – both those already built up, which you as purchaser will want to see adequately financed, and those which will be added during your future ownership.

Pensions are also complex. It is quite common for the pension figures to be the very last item to be finally resolved after an acquisition.

It is unwise to sign an agreement on any technical subject without consulting an expert. In the case of pensions this usually means an actuary. If pension problems are not identified until after the agreement has been signed then there will be long and expensive arguments to follow. It is much cheaper in the long run to bring in an actuary sufficiently early to forestall conflict before it actually happens. If you are buying a 'people business' the actuary's advice may be as crucial to the outcome of the whole deal as that of your accountant or lawyer.

At the time of writing (June 1988) the last elements of a revolution in pensions are just coming into being. In this chapter I have tried to foresee some of the effects that revolution will have on company acquisitions. But the psychological consequences of the new pensions regime will be far-reaching – there may be surprises in store for all of us.

What is a pension scheme?

A pension scheme is a promise to pay. However that promise is defined – and it can be quite simple or very complicated – the essence is that the employer promises the members that pensions will be paid many years in the future. These promises are the *liabilities* of the pension scheme.

But promises can be broken. In a takeover employees will naturally be worried that promises already made, but relating to events in the future, may not be honoured. The Occupational Pensions Board has recently been instructed to investigate such situations and to make recommendations on possible changes in the law.

The purchaser may decide to meet his predecessor's promises, or may modify them for any one of a number of reasons. Either way, the ability to meet the original or modified promises will come from a combination of four sources:

1. the assets already set aside by the vendor towards pensions,
2. any further payment from the vendor which may be specified in the sale agreement,
3. money which the purchaser is able to set aside out of the future profits of the acquired company,
4. money available in the future from other sources, e.g. the profits of other companies within the purchaser's group.

Items (3) and (4) are outside the scope of this chapter. So let us start by looking at (1). At the extreme there may be nothing set aside at all: this is called an unfunded pension scheme. The most common example is a pension promise contained in a service contract, where quite often the employer has made no financial provision for the contractual liability.

However, most pension schemes in the UK are set up under trust. The intention here is to set aside a sum of money which will be used for employees' pensions and associated benefits, irrespective of the future well-being (or even existence) of the sponsoring employer. From the point of view of the employees this protection is valuable, though in acquisition situations far from complete.

Pension scheme trustees have different responsibilities from those of the employer. Each employer should therefore consult his trustees early in the negotiations to avoid problems later. This applies whether the trustees are directors of the company, trade union nominees or an external body such as a bank trust company. Even if the trustees are exactly the same people as the Board of the company they must still act, in relation to the pension fund, with the scheme members' interests uppermost in their minds. If they do not, they will risk action for breach of trust.

Different kinds of pension

Most UK pension schemes are of the *final salary* type. Here it is the *benefits* which are defined. The employees' contributions are also fixed, but the employer's contributions are not – he pays whatever is required to make up the balance of the cost of benefits. This balance can vary considerably over the years, depending on the experience of the scheme.

A final salary scheme provides (so long as it continues) security in retirement for the members. The reverse of this coin is that there is an open-ended liability for the employer. It is the open-endedness which makes the treatment of pensions in an acquisition a matter for negotiation rather than fact.

The alternative, of course, is a scheme in which the *contributions* are defined (and the eventual pensions are uncertain). This is called a *money purchase* pension scheme and fits closely with the idea of pensions as 'deferred pay'. Each year a contribution of a specified amount – often a fixed percentage of salary – is set aside and used for pension provision. The whole thing is very simple and one does not have the cross-subsidies which exist below the surface in every final salary pension scheme.

Recent legislation, principally the Social Security Act 1986, was designed to encourage pension provision along money purchase lines. In an acquisition context this will have two main effects:

1. It will be more common, especially when buying a small company, to find that it has a simple money purchase scheme in force. Here the purchaser is faced with a relatively straightforward decision: Am I prepared to maintain the contribution promise which has already been given to employees?

   Usually the promise will be based on a simple percentage of salary/earnings but occasionally one will find a scheme in which the input depends in some way on profit-sharing bonuses. In this case pensions are more intricately bound up with the company's whole remuneration structure so any proposed changes in that structure will need to take pensions carefully into account. Employees will be conscious of this and may seek early reassurance as to the purchaser's intentions.

2. Some employers – mainly the larger ones – will have introduced money purchase elements into an existing final salary pension scheme. There are various ways of doing this, most of them involving a high degree of complexity and an increased need for efficient administration procedures. Expert actuarial advice is essential in assessing the possible range of costs of 'hybrid' schemes of this kind.

Contracting out of SERPS

Since 1978 State pension provision has been in two parts. The State Basic Pension is available to all employees, subject to an adequate National Insurance contribution record. The second tier is the State Earnings

Related Pension Scheme or SERPS. This provides an additional pension based on an employee's career earnings record from 1978 onwards.

Companies can, if they wish, arrange for their employees to be 'contracted out' of SERPS so long as the company pension scheme meets certain conditions. In this event both the employer and the employees pay a lower rate of National Insurance contributions in return for replacing part of the SERPS pension by way of the company scheme. Until April 1988 this was an all-or-nothing decision – a whole category of employees was either contracted out or contracted in. However, as we shall see in a moment, the position has now changed radically.

'1988 and all that'

The Social Security Act 1986, effective from 1988, has completely reshaped UK pensions. The major new elements are these:

1. Pension scheme membership can no longer be made a condition of employment. Employees are free to leave (or refuse to join) the employer's pension scheme if they wish.
2. Employees can provide for their retirement by new Personal Pension (PP) contracts of various kinds. Employers may contribute to such contracts but there is no compulsion to do so. A few employers are encouraging their employees to use particular PP contracts.
3. Employers can offer a new kind of pension scheme, called a Contracted Out Money Purchase Scheme or COMP, to enable employees to contract out of SERPS without giving them final salary pension commitment.
4. Personal Pensions may also be used by an employee to contract out of SERPS individually on a money purchase basis. Originally this facility was to be available only for employees not in a pension scheme. At the last minute the government conceded that employees in a contracted-in pension scheme could also have PPs.
5. The government will in certain circumstances make extra 'incentive' payments to PPs and COMPs, until April 1993, to encourage contracting out of SERPS.
6. All pension schemes must offer an Additional Voluntary Contribution (AVC) facility. Members can also invest in new Free-Standing AVC (FSAVC) contracts of their own choice.
7. SERPS benefits are reduced for employees retiring in the year 2000 or later.

In the light of (1) above, employers have had to reconsider the eligibility conditions for their pension schemes. Many have told employees that, having once decided to opt out (or refused to join), they will not be able to re-enter later. Others will allow a change of mind at intervals of five years, or at any time up to the age of 40, etc. This means that a purchaser must look carefully at the *non*-members of the pension scheme. If they have been given rights to join or re-join later these rights must be taken into account as they will affect the future operations and cost of the scheme.

Pot of gold or can of worms?

Partly because of the long timescale, it is usual to set aside a fund of money towards pension liabilities. This fund constitutes the *assets* of the scheme. But no one has a crystal ball to tell the employer exactly how much to set aside out of current profits. The actuary can recommend a rate of contributions, and advise on the risks of any given course of action, but in a final salary scheme the only certainty is that his estimates will be wrong one way or the other.

The actuary's calculations are based on an extremely simple and obvious relationship:

$$
\begin{array}{ccc}
\text{Value} & \text{Value} & \text{Value of} \\
\text{of} \quad - & \text{of} \quad = & \text{future} \\
\text{liabilities} & \text{assets} & \text{contributions}
\end{array}
$$

To put it another way, the cost of the promises made has to be supported by two sums of money: one which is already set aside (and which will go on producing income in the future) and one which has not been set aside yet.

Note that all three items in the equation are unknown. The value of the liabilities will depend upon future years' salaries; future income from the assets cannot be predicted with certainty, and the terms on which it will be reinvested are still less predictable; and of course you cannot guarantee that the company will be in a position to make contributions at a given level in the future.

The equation can also be turned on its head so that the liabilities become the balancing item – the employer would then be saying to the actuary: 'This is what I can afford to pay for the foreseeable future. What benefits can I provide in return?' The result may be that promises previously given in good faith have to be cut back.

Two employers with similar pension liabilities can have entirely different levels of asset backing in their pension schemes – from 50 to 200 per cent of the liabilities, say. From your point of view, as a potential purchaser, a 200 per cent scheme is a pot of gold and may well fund a good part of the purchase price of the target company. A 50 per cent-funded scheme is a can of worms and you may either wish to negotiate a lower purchase price for the business, or find a way of cutting back on the promised level of pensions.

Surpluses

This brings us to the question of surpluses. It is important to understand that, in a continuing final salary pension scheme, the surplus is a matter of opinion rather than of fact. A change in perceptions of the future, or an unforeseen change in membership, e.g. through a redundancy programme, can lead to the disappearance or doubling of a stated surplus.

In assessing the surplus the actuary's opinion will be affected by what is known of the prospects of the client company's employees. If the actuary honestly believes the company can thrive, then the expected rates of salary increase may be higher (and the expected redundancies lower) than otherwise. This will increase the value of benefits and so reduce the surplus.

The government has legislated to prevent what it sees as unacceptable levels of surplus from building up in tax-free pension funds and the Finance Act 1986 requires such unacceptable surpluses to be run off over a relatively short period – usually five years, a very short time in the life of a pension scheme. For this reason the level of surplus will often be changing very much more rapidly than it would ever have done in the past. A pension fund whose actuarial valuation last year showed a surplus of £1,000,000 may easily have reduced that figure to £500,000, or even gone into deficit, by the time you are reading the report. It is therefore essential that you get up-to-date figures rather than rely on existing ones.

How does the state of a pension fund impinge on the sale agreement? This, of course, is an agreement *between two companies*. But the amount available from the vendor's pension scheme is governed solely by that scheme's trust deed. It is most unlikely that this will by itself produce exactly the result which the vendor and purchaser companies would achieve in their negotiations. So they will need to insert some additional provisions into the sale agreement regarding a balancing or 'shortfall' payment.

This was well-named when most pension funds were in deficit as it then involved a payment from the vendor to the purchaser (or equivalently, a reduction in the purchase price paid). When the pension fund is in surplus the payment will go the other way, i.e. the purchaser is paying more to acquire a company with a surplus in its pension scheme than would otherwise be paid. Naturally the purchaser will do everything possible to resist the vendor's suggestion of this extra payment!

Accounting for pensions

It may be your intention, provisionally at least, to maintain the existing pension scheme of the target company. You will obviously need to put something into your budget to allow for the cost of pension provision and it is tempting just to use the percentage contribution rate which was paid to that pension scheme in the past. However this is unlikely to be a good guide to the true costs of providing pensions in future. There are various reasons for this. For example, the distribution of employees by age/sex/past service/category of employment may be quite different under your management from what it was before. This may arise through redundancies, or more gradually as you reshape the company and perhaps reposition it in the labour market.

There is a another danger area here: the treatment of pension contributions in the company's accounts. Up to now it has been usual for companies to put in their accounts only the amount actually paid into the pension scheme. So, for example, if the company was taking a contribution 'holiday' there would be a zero pension cost in the accounts.

Like so many other aspects of pensions, this is about to change. The accountancy bodies have issued a new Statement of Standard Accounting Practice (SSAP24: Accounting for Pensions) which requires a different treatment for accounting periods beginning after 1 July 1988. Company accounts will have to show a cost based on the pensions which employees are accruing each year, regardless of whether the company is actually paying contributions or not. The way this will work in practice means that companies will sometimes find themselves with a large balance-sheet provision for pension contributions, which was not there in past years and which will change in quite complex ways over the next few years. You may well need to ask your accountant and your actuary to liaise in interpreting the vendor's accounts.

Can the past and future liabilities be separated?

Leaving aside the question of what actuarial assumptions are to be used, there are two main ways in which the pre-acquisition liabilities can be assessed. These correspond in principle to different methods of valuing a company.

The more usual, and perhaps more obvious, method corresponds to valuing a company in line with its assets. First, one calculates the pensions which members have accrued up to the date of acquisition. Next a capital value is placed on all these accrued pensions. The result is compared with the value of the pension scheme's investments.

The other approach is to look at the whole of each member's pension (not just the part relating to pre-acquisition service) and assess the contribution rate required to support those pensions. Deduct the existing contribution rate, capitalise the difference, and the result is the shortfall figure. This is consistent with valuing a company in terms of its profit record. In effect, the purchaser is saying, 'Your profit history does not adequately recognise the true cost of the pension scheme, because you have not paid enough into it out of your profits. I will therefore have to pay in more out of future profits, and the calculation must take this into account.'

This second method has its theoretical attractions, but as we have already seen, the current rate of contributions can be distorted for many reasons. Moreover, if your intention is to amend the level of benefits substantially, the contribution rate for the present benefits is neither here nor there. So in the majority of cases the 'assets' method is likely to be more appropriate.

Insured schemes

Thirty years ago most pension schemes, whether final salary or money purchase, were arranged through insurance companies. Only the biggest employers ran their own 'self-administered' schemes. Those days are long gone. Now only smaller companies are likely to run 'insured' pension schemes, at least as far as final salary schemes are concerned.

It is important to realise that insurance here is merely a form of investment – it does not provide any protection against the biggest risk to a final salary pension scheme, namely the possibility that members' salaries (on which the eventual benefits will be based) will go out of control. This happened in the inflationary mid-1970s and only an optimist would say that it could never happen again.

Buying a company with an insured pension scheme presents some extra difficulties. The insurance company is an additional party involved in the sale process and it may be advisable to seek the insurer's views on whatever is proposed, especially if, as is often the case, the policy gives the insurer wide discretion over the amount to be paid if the policy is surrendered. The trouble is that there is no natural termination point of a group pension policy. For this reason, and others, it may not be at all easy to put a value on the insurance policy for the purposes of the sale agreement. Once again your actuary will need to be involved – not least to negotiate with the insurance company's actuary!

The pension clause of the sale agreement

The pension clause must cover the treatment of pension rights earned up to the acquisition date. It should lay down how those rights are to be valued, and also the value to be put upon the assets (investments) backing them. If the assets and liabilities are unequal it should specify whether the two companies are to make a balancing payment either way, and the tax treatment of that 'shortfall' payment.

Usually it is impossible to finalise these calculations before completion. It is essential, therefore, to make the sale agreement as specific as possible on pensions, and to avoid ambiguity. Any differences of interpretation can lead to time-consuming renegotiation after the event.

One point on which it can be particularly difficult to agree is the treatment of pension increases after retirement. These are often granted on a discretionary basis, i.e. not promised in the pension scheme rules. But if there have been regular increases in the past, members will expect them to continue and the purchaser will wish the calculations to allow for this. The vendor, on the other hand, will wish to limit the liability to a strict interpretation of the rules. The new accounting standards will tend to favour the purchaser's view here.

As well as these important points of principle, the pensions clause should cover a number of practical matters, including:

1. the arrangements for calculating and verifying the amounts to be paid, including any shortfall payment between the two companies,
2. the precise definition of which employees are covered by the agreement, and the position of any who are not (e.g. those to be made redundant),
3. the way in which members are to be notified of what is happening to their pension rights, and by whom,
4. the responsibility for liaising with the statutory authorities, viz. the Inland Revenue, the Occupational Pensions Board and the DHSS.

The vendor may also ask you to give assurances about the future, e.g. a promise that the pension scheme will not be altered in any way. This should be resisted. The vendor will certainly have had the right to amend his own pension scheme and there is no reason why that right should not pass to you.

Taxation

Pension schemes are very nearly tax-free. Employers' and employees' contributions are relieved from Corporation Tax and Income Tax respectively, and investment proceeds, both income and capital gains, are payable gross. Admittedly, the pensions emerging are taxed in the pensioner's hands as earned income, though even here the member can exchange part of the pension for a tax-free lump-sum at retirement;

refunds paid to short-service leavers are currently taxed at 20 per cent; the occasional pension fund may be assessed to tax on trading profits; and refunds of surplus to an employer are taxed at 40 per cent. But by and large, despite some encroachments in recent years by the Inland Revenue, pension schemes still operate largely in a tax-free environment.

However this does *not* mean that you can ignore tax when considering the purchase of a company with a pension fund. It is very relevant in relation to a shortfall payment.

For example, suppose that the company you are buying has a pension scheme with assets of £1 million, but that the agreed value of the past service liabilities is £1½ million. The vendor may object to making a shortfall payment of the full £500,000 to the purchaser, since it would be regarded by the Inland Revenue as a capital payment and so ineligible for Corporation Tax relief. It the vendor had made up the deficit by increased regular contributions in the future, or by a special contribution to the scheme, full tax relief would have been available. Moreover, when the purchaser puts the money into the scheme tax relief is available.

So long as both companies are in the same taxable position, therefore, it would seem fair to specify that the shortfall payment should be made net of Corporation Tax at the current rate, so that deducting tax at 35 per cent the £500,000 would be reduced to £325,000.

If the tax position of the two companies is different, there will need to be negotiations with a view to agreeing a notional tax rate for the purpose of this calculation.

Disclosure

Pension schemes generate large quantities of paper. You will want to ensure that all relevant documents are disclosed to you. This will often be authorised by a general reference either in the pensions clause itself, or in the warranties section of the Sale Agreement.

But what documents should you actually ask for? The following checklist may be helpful:

1. Trust Deed and Rules and any amendments thereto.
2. Details of any benefit changes which have not yet been formally documented in 1.
3. Explanatory booklet and any other material issued to members – announcement of benefit changes, sample annual benefit statement, etc.
4. Latest actuarial valuation report.
5. Confirmation that scheme has received final tax approval under Finance Act 1970 (now Income & Corporation Taxes Act 1988).

6. If contracted-out, current contracting-out certificate from the Occupational Pensions Board, also the supporting 'Certificate A' signed
   by the scheme's actuary.
7. Full details of assets, including copies of insurance policies if
   applicable.
8. Details of insurance arrangements for death-in-service benefits.
9. Latest membership listing, showing accrued and potential benefits
   for each member as well as ages, pensionable salaries, etc.
10. Details of any material changes which have occurred, or have been
    promised, in relation to any of the above items.
11. Details of administration arrangements, including computer systems
    used (if any), contracts with external administrators, etc.
12. Latest report from Trustees to members.
13. Latest accounts of the scheme if more recent than those included in
    12 above.
14. Rights granted to non-members to join (or rejoin) the scheme at a
    later date.

Strategy

To integrate or not to integrate

One thing the purchaser must consider as early as possible is whether,
in the long term, to assimilate the transferring employees so that their
benefits correspond with those of existing employees. This is probably
the most fundamental decision of all. Do you wish to have one pension
scheme covering all the employees of your enlarged group, or do you
wish to keep the 'old' and 'new' employees separate? If the two groups
do the same kind of work, in the same part of the country, then probably
they will quite soon feel like a single organisation and lose their separate
identities. Clearly, it will make sense in the circumstances to harmonise all
employee benefits. If, on the other hand, the two groups are in different
industries, different parts of the country and different unions, then there
is a lot to be said for retaining separate benefits, and, in particular,
separate pension arrangements. Moreover, if you have any thoughts that
one day you might wish to sell your newly acquired subsidiary, keeping
its pension scheme separate will avoid many potential complications.

Cost of levelling up benefits

Let us assume that you have decided to integrate. You need to design a
unified pension scheme to keep both the 'old' and 'new' employees happy.
If one pension scheme is much more generous than the other then there

is undoubtedly going to be pressure for a levelling-up. The cost of any levelling-up items will fall solely on the purchaser, and can easily amount to several percentage points of his total yearly payroll.

Even where the two pension schemes have similar overall costs the pressures for levelling up still exist. The problem is that employees will tend to look at each component of the benefits as a separate item. To give a simple example, one group may be pressing for its death-in-service benefits to be increased while the other casts envious eyes at the first group's higher level of retirement pensions.

Everybody wants the best of both worlds. Once we start analysing the two schemes into their component parts:

Pensionable salary	Widows' pensions in retirement
Final pensionable salary	Death-in-service benefits
Pensionable service	Employees' contributions
Pension increases	etc.

all employees will be able to find some aspect in which their benefits could – and in their opinion should – be improved. There is no simple answer to these pressures for levelling up. It is a matter of compromise between the desires of the employees and what the employer can afford. Sometimes the best solution is to create a new pension scheme, with some features drawn from each of the existing schemes, and then invite employees to transfer to the new scheme at their own option.

Do not forget the problems of administration. If you decide to run two schemes there will undoubtedly be many points of detail, and of definition, in which they differ. The more such differences exist, the more time and manpower will be needed to carry out the administration function.

Non-pensionable employees

The value of an employment benefit, as perceived by the employee, is not the same thing as the cost to the employer of providing it.

This obvious fact has some important implications. Suppose that you have acquired a group of employees whose employment is non-pensionable or whose pension benefits are minimal. This potentially difficult situation can sometimes be defused by providing them at an early stage with substantial death-in-service benefits, e.g. a lump-sum of two years' earnings. This will usually cost less than 1 per cent of payroll but may be appreciated by the employees as much as a pension, which would have cost the employer 10 per cent of payroll!

Note also that the Social Security Act 1986 creates several attractive new ways of providing pensions for such employees at very low cost to the employer.

Redundancies

Sometimes the purchaser and the vendor agree that certain groups of employees will be made redundant either shortly before or shortly after the takeover.

In the past, 'early leavers' have tended to get a poor deal from final salary pension schemes. Often a scheme makes no distinction in benefit rights between those who leave of their own accord and those made redundant. So a redundancy programme will lead to a windfall profit in the pension scheme. Successive legislation, however, has led to a gradual improvement in leavers' pension rights and the profits accruing to the scheme are often much less material than they used to be.

As purchaser, you have to weigh up these pension scheme profits against two non-financial items: the employee-relations consequences of being seen to cause redundancies, and the administrative burden of numerous pension calculations. You may also be asked to put in the sale agreement an assurance that the transferred employees will be treated favourably in the event of later redundancy, e.g. within two years of the acquisition. This is not unreasonable and may help to mitigate the natural apprehension felt by members and their trade unions. However, complying with such a commitment can sometimes require complicated administrative procedures which you will want to avoid.

Note that, in certain defined circumstances, a statutory redundancy payment may be reduced to reflect the payment of an immediate pension.

Conclusion

The main themes of this chapter can perhaps best be summarised in the form of a checklist. And keeping the following points in mind will considerably reduce the risk of post-acquisition problems.

1. Do not make promises without thinking them through – they can later turn out to be expensive or difficult to administer.
2. Insist on getting as much information as possible, as early as possible.
3. Take actuarial advice at an early stage, and involve the actuary in devising the pensions part of the agreement.
4. If the pension scheme is in deficit, can you insist on a shortfall payment? If in surplus, can you resist it? In either case remember to consider Corporation Tax on the payment.
5. Ensure that the agreement is specific about pensions. Minimise the scope for differences of interpretation.
6. Ensure that you know exactly which pensions are to become your

responsibility, including those for employees who have already retired and those with preserved pensions.

7. Take into account all pension promises, including those in service contracts, and any unfunded pension scheme.
8. If a transfer of assets is to be made to your own scheme, consider whether the assets of the vendor's scheme are in a convenient form for you to accept. Would you prefer a cash transfer instead?
9. What benefits are you going to provide for the transferring employees? What level of contributions will be required?
10. Will you aim to integrate the old and new pension schemes? What is the cost of any levelling-up?
11. Ascertain the views of your own pension scheme's trustees on any changes which may affect that scheme's finances or membership.

Incentive arrangements
Why have incentive schemes?

Having bought a company, you will obviously want to get the very best out of all its employees, whether senior or junior. And there will probably be certain key people whose services you cannot afford to lose. While encouragement and leadership may help to achieve these goals, financial incentives usually have greater impact.

Deciding what kind of financial incentive to offer is not straightforward. There are many possibilities to consider. You may also be faced with the problem of extending incentive schemes from your existing company into your new acquisition, or even of rationalising two completely different sets of incentives operating in the two companies.

Cash schemes

A share of the company's profits, paid annually in cash, is attractive to employees at all levels and can help to make them aware of the need to make the company profitable. But it is important to select a measure of profitability to which employees can readily relate, and preferably one which is available to them, such as profit before tax on ordinary activities. A case can always be made for adjusting a profit figure to include this or to exclude that in the interests of fairness but a system will be counter-productive if it delights the chief accountant at the expense of baffling the average employee.

While it is easy to introduce a bonus system, it is not so easy to make sure that it continues to motivate. Systems have often had to be scrapped after a few years because they were producing anomalous results. The most important thing is to set a *norm* or *target* of performance which has to be reached before a bonus is paid. This is much fairer to shareholders and is itself a strong motivator, particularly if the bonus depends on the extent to which the target has been exceeded. In setting the target, bear in mind that:

1. A norm which is fixed rigidly at the outset will rapidly go out of date as circumstances change. If a norm is derived from a particularly profitable period of the company's history, then it may in future deny incentive bonuses to participants who have in fact performed very well in different circumstances.
2. To avoid this problem, companies often take the previous year's performance as the target. However, any bonus system which requires perpetual improvements creates an unfortunate treadmill effect. Participants can be more successful but achieve less and less bonus. If performance levels out, even at a very satisfactory high level, then no bonus will be paid.
3. Many bonus systems are designed around budgets which are set annually. While this can be made to work, the process of target-setting is difficult and may be destructive of team spirit, quite apart from the obvious dangers of 'feedback' between the budgeting process and the bonus system.

These difficulties can be overcome, with care. Designing the right scheme is not as simple as it appears and it can be well worth paying for professional advice.

When it comes to motivating a senior manager, bonuses need to be related in some way to the results of the operation under his direct control. It is crucial to select the right measure of profit-centre performance. Often two or more measures such as profit and turnover, or ratios such as returns on capital and profit margin, can be combined to advantage.

Profit-related Pay

Profit-related Pay (PRP) was introduced in the Finance (No. 2) Act 1987. It is designed to encourage a company to modify, or even abandon, annual pay bargaining and substitute a flexible profit-related bonus system. Tax relief for the employees is provided with a view to securing their acceptance of this.

PRP could be particularly helpful to the company with low profitability but, paradoxically, it is those companies which will find it most difficult to install. Consider the ratio of profit to employee pay in a company. If profits are twice pay, a bonus of 5 per cent of pay will cost the equivalent of 2½ per cent of profits. On the other hand, if profits are only a quarter of the pay bill, a bonus of 5 per cent of pay will cost 20 per cent of profits.

The PRP scheme cannot be approved for tax relief unless it will pay out a 5 per cent bonus when profit is the same as in the base year. It follows that it is mainly companies with a high profit to pay ratio which will be able to concentrate on using PRP as a tax-relieved form of cash profit-sharing. Such companies are unlikely to have to contemplate cost-cutting in order to pay for the PRP bonus.

Companies where profit is a relatively small proportion of the employee pay bill, on the other hand, will be forced into drastic cost-cutting if they wish to use PRP. To use PRP realistically such a company must either increase its revenue faster than inflation (without commensurate cost increases), or actually reduce costs – perhaps by introducing PRP partly in place of normal pay increases. The latter was, of course, the government's intention. Companies by and large have not been prepared to go through the disruption of using PRP in this way but in the case of a newly acquired company it may be feasible.

Share schemes

Cash bonus systems can provide a good incentive in the short term. For longer-term motivation a scheme based on company shares or share options is more appropriate. There are three basic forms of tax-efficient share scheme.

Profit-sharing share schemes

These were introduced by the Finance Act 1978. They are company-wide schemes in which all full-time employees (those working 25 hours or more per week) who have completed five years' service must be eligible to participate. The company nominates Trustees and pays over to them any money required to acquire its shares on behalf of the participants.

Shares are appropriated to all participants, who may not dispose of them for at least two years except on death, retirement, disability or redundancy. In return for complying with these rules, the employer obtains Corporation Tax relief on the money used by the Trustees to acquire shares. Moreover the participating employee is not subject to Income Tax on the value of the shares so long as he leaves the shares with the Trustees for at least five years after they are appropriated to him. Capital Gains Tax does apply on a sale, but the annual CGT exemption will often wipe this out.

The maximum which may be appropriated to an employee in any one tax year is £1,250 or, if greater, 10 per cent of his taxable earnings with an overriding limit of £5,000.

Savings-related share option schemes

These were introduced in their present form by the Finance Act 1980. They too must be company-wide schemes. Employees who wish to participate must first enter into a SAYE contract with a building society or the Department for National Savings. They are then granted options to buy shares in the company, to be paid for out of the proceeds of the SAYE contract.

The aggregate contributions by any one employee must be between £10 and £100 per month, and must continue for at least five years. The option price is based on the market value of the shares at the time the option is granted. Participants are not liable to Income Tax on the gain (except in limited circumstances arising from a takeover or company reconstruction) and, as in the case of profit-sharing share schemes, Capital Gains Tax will often be completely offset within the annual exemption limit.

Executive share option schemes

These were introduced by the Finance Act 1984. The name is really a misnomer. Although usually granted to employees at management level, executive share options may in theory apply to any employee working at least 20 hours per week (25 hours for directors).

Here a company can be selective as to who participates and to what extent. The option price is based on the market value of the shares at the date of grant, and the participant may be granted options up to a cumulative total value of £100,000 or, if greater, four times annual earnings.

Option gains are subject to Capital Gains Tax when exercised, but the participant is not subject to Income Tax as long as the option is exercised in the period between three and ten years after the date of grant. A three-year interval must elapse between tax-relieved exercises of options.

Choosing the right kind of scheme

Profit-sharing share schemes are still arguably the best means of putting shares into your employees' hands. The five-year lock-in period for Income Tax relief has proved to be an extremely effective way of getting employees used to the concept of share ownership. Any steps to encourage everyone to pull in the same direction will be of great benefit to the company and its shareholders. If, on the other hand, selectivity is essential then consider executive share options.

Savings-related share option schemes are less popular than they were when interest rates were very high. Nevertheless, they still provide the potential for tax-relieved capital gains and should certainly not be ignored.

Shares used in all tax-approved share schemes must:

1. be part of the ordinary share capital,
2. be fully paid and not redeemable,
3. not be subject to restrictions which do not apply to all shares of the same class (except that you may impose certain restrictions on shareholders who leave your employment),
4. be either:
   (a) quoted shares or
   (b) unquoted shares in a company which is not under the control of another company or
   (c) unquoted shares in a company which is under the control of a non-close quoted company.

There are many other detailed requirements contained in the legislation. Moreover, if the acquiring company is a *quoted* company, there are numerous additional restrictions imposed by committees representing institutional investors.

In view of 4 above, it will often be impossible to use the shares of a subsidiary company in a tax-approved share scheme. If your private company has acquired another private company you will either have to use the parent company's shares or adopt an unapproved scheme.

So much for share schemes. In some circumstances you may be unable to use share schemes at all, e.g. because your Articles of Association do not comply with the legislative requirements. Equally, you may be able but unwilling to offer shares. In these circumstances a cash scheme and/or PRP should be considered.

One of the most attractive combinations, where shares are available, is a share scheme with a cash alternative. The employee can give up his right to the allocated shares in the expectation of receiving immediate cash instead.

Bringing the new company into your existing incentive schemes

An incentive scheme designed for one company may not be appropriate for another company. Bringing the two companies together in a single group will not alter this fact.

If, for example, you are pursuing a policy of 'vertical integration' the two businesses will be operating in different parts of the same industry – one in production, perhaps, and the other in distribution. The measure of performance which is suitable for one company will not be right for the other and it is essential to take this into account in any incentive arrangements.

Dilution can be a problem too. Suppose company A regularly shares a percentage of profit amongst its employees. If company B is less profitable, and is brought into this system immediately, then bonuses in company A will suffer.

There are two possible solutions to consider. If company B is capable of being brought up to company A's profitability ratio (profit divided by payroll) then wait for a year or two before extending the incentive system to company B. In the interim period a *notional* past performance record, based on company A's performance, could perhaps be used.

If by its nature company B's ratio will always be lower, on the other hand, it will need to have its own incentive criteria.

This does not mean that there should be no common elements. Indeed, it is important psychologically that the incentive arrangements should recognise common ownership. This can best be met by including some element of 'group' performance in the incentive arrangements, especially for senior management. This will help them to appreciate that, while their prime responsibility is for their particular company, the various companies are all working towards a common goal, i.e. the greater profitability of the group.

The inclusion of a group element inevitably means that managers will sometimes get a bonus even when their own company's performance has been poor; and conversely that exceptionally good performance may not be rewarded in full. While it is understandable that individuals may have reservations about this – especially those in the latter category! – they will usually agree in the end that it makes sense. After all, what is the meaning of a group of companies if each company is not to share to some extent in the ups and downs of the others?

What if your target company already has a share scheme?

If your new company is operating a share scheme at the time you acquire it, there are some important implications which you ignore at your cost.

First, if there is an option scheme, it will almost certainly provide for the options to be exercised in the event of a change of control. You will therefore have to take these new shares into account when negotiating the terms of the acquisition – substantial numbers could be involved. You have the choice, of course, of merely leaving these shares in the hands of the managers as minority holdings, but this may not suit you, and anyway would be demotivating because of the greatly reduced status of the shares.

Alternatively, the option scheme may contain clauses which allow options to 'roll over' into options over shares in your acquiring company. There is no question of this being forced upon you so it will be a matter for you to decide – and you do not have to have an option scheme of your own to put this arrangement into effect. If you decide not to roll the options over, the likelihood is that they will be exercised and the preceding paragraph will then apply.

If the new company's scheme is a profit-sharing one, the position is more complicated and professional advice will be essential. In essence, there are three possibilities:

1. If the acquisition is on a *shares for shares* basis only, the new shares in your company will replace the old shares in the trust and it could be some years before they vest in the participants.
2. If the deal is on a *part-shares, part-cash* basis then 1 applies but the cash is dealt with as a 'capital receipt' with special tax treatment.
3. If the acquisition is purely *cash for shares*, then the participants in the share scheme can instruct the trustees to sell their shares to you (however recently they were appropriated under the trust) and take the cash straight away. There will be some Income Tax consequences for the participants but these are likely, in the circumstances, to be relatively minor.

Some final points to consider

Transfer pricing

Difficulties can arise where one company in the group has material trading relationships with another. If the parent company's Board can now adjust the profitability of company A by varying the price at which it sells its product to company B, then profit will no longer be a suitable measure of company A's success. If the existing arrangement is left unaltered, company A's management will quickly become demotivated as they realise that their bonuses are no longer the result of their own decisions.

To overcome this, from the point of view of incentive schemes, it is necessary either to compute the notional profits which would have arisen in the absence of transfer pricing or, more usually, to relate all incentives to the performance of the group as a whole and ignore the contribution made by each profit centre individually.

Triggers

Another frequent pitfall relates to executive share options triggered by particular levels of performance. If the triggers are such that options are granted only in good years, then the option price, being based on market value, will inevitably be high. It is much better to *grant* options regardless of performance but to retain the incentive element by requiring certain performance criteria ('triggers') to be met before the options can be *exercised*.

Unapproved schemes

It is easy to forget that tax approval is not always essential for a share scheme. In certain circumstances an unapproved share option scheme can be an attractive alternative, especially in a private company. In the past private companies have often avoided share option schemes because they were not prepared to make the necessary changes to ownership structure or to their Articles of Association. Following the Capital Gains Tax changes in the 1988 Budget, however, the use of an unapproved scheme is now a much less unattractive alternative.

Deferred bonuses

Most companies at some stage face the problem of how to retain the services of their rising younger executives and managers. It is worth looking at whether part of a bonus should be granted on a deferred basis – nominally earned now but payable, subject to certain conditions, at a future date. Deferment of bonuses has a number of significant advantages:

1. It provides a golden handcuff to discourage young and capable executives from leaving to take up another post, since part of the bonus will be forfeited if they leave other than in the usual compassionate circumstances such as death, retirement, injury, etc. Indeed, there must be some risk of forfeiture if there is to be a deferment of the income tax liability.
2. Where bonuses are likely to fluctuate deferment can create a smoothing effect, making domestic planning easier for the individual.
3. There can be an element of security in deferment, for a deceased or redundant executive will have cash in the pipeline which may escape tax in the former case and will probably incur a lower tax liability in the latter case.

4. Deferred bonuses can be designed to be drawn upon at the time of exercising an option. This is not particularly tax-efficient but it does enable the executive to retain more of the shares than would otherwise have been the case. This can be particularly useful in private companies, where there is no ready market for the shares, or in cases where the balance of control is delicate.

Non-marketability

In private companies the use of share schemes may cause difficulties because of the lack of a market in the shares. The problem can be mitigated by establishing a so-called warehouse trust. The trust is funded by loans (internal or external) and operates as a buyer of last resort.

Pension planning

Finally, incentives and pensions need not be considered in isolation from each other. It can be very attractive to make use of bonuses in pension planning.

It has long been possible for employees and directors to divert part or all of a bonus into some kind of pension arrangement (usually a simple money purchase arrangement so that there is no further commitment from the company). In the past it has been necessary to arrange this by way of a 'bonus sacrifice' which needed careful documentation, especially where the amount was large and the bonus was contractual. The alternative was for the employee to receive the bonus, and then invest it towards his retirement by way of an additional voluntary contribution (AVC) but this was unattractive owing to the Inland Revenue requirement that AVCs be continued on a uniform basis for at least five years.

However, the five-year requirement was relaxed in 1987 and pension scheme trustees may now accept irregular or single payments. The introduction of 'Free Standing Additional Voluntary Contributions' schemes means that there is also a much wider range of investment media available to the employee. These two facts should mean a considerable increase in the next few years in the use of bonuses for pension planning.

Acknowledgement

I should like to thank my colleague Stephen Collins for his extensive assistance with the Incentives sections of this chapter.

Chapter 8

The importance of public relations

MARTIN WRAY

Associate, City & Corporate Counsel

Introduction

Well, what about public relations? It's a fair question. Do public relations really matter when buying a company? If so, why, when and how do they matter? What can good PR do to help the deal? Can bad PR hinder the deal or even frustrate it? Need PR be expensive? This chapter seeks to answer these questions, and to provide guidance on the techniques involved in achieving good PR for the acquisition.

PR, however good, cannot turn a bad deal into a good one. PR is essentially no more than a very useful tool – a trowel, perhaps, is the best analogy. It can smooth the deal at every stage of its progress, and it can help to enhance your company's reputation as a result of the acquisition. But it is only a tool. A trowel cannot smooth things by itself. It depends on the skill of the hand that holds it.

When and where to begin PR

At the very beginning! Or at least as soon as the deal is more than just a gleam in the eye.

If you have a PR department or spokesperson, involve them in confidence from the outset. Their main task is to avoid surprises. But they cannot do their job if they are constantly surprised by the company itself.

If you don't have an in-house PR function, decide early on who is going to speak for the company. It may need to be the chief executive or the finance director. Who speaks for the company is not really the crucial issue. What is crucial is to avoid a tower of babel – many people speaking many tongues! That way lies potential disaster!

Now you have a spokesperson. What is going to be said, to whom and when? Start with an *apparently* simple question: 'Why are we buying this company?' The answer may turn out to be more complicated than you think, but debating and agreeing the answer within the company is the key for successful PR in all its subsequent stages.

So why are you buying the company? Try to condense your reasons to a few sentences and make them positive. The reasons can obviously be manifold. Here are a few examples:

1. This deal will increase company X's market share in the UK widget market by X per cent. (Don't forget the competition policy aspects! See Chapter 6 on legal aspects.)
2. This deal provides an excellent opportunity for company X to expand into the widgets-*related* market.
3. This deal provides the opportunity to pool the research resources of company X and company Y to the benefit of both companies, their shareholders and their employees.
4. This deal achieves company X's ambition to secure a base for expansion in the key overseas market of [USA, Japan, Europe].
5. This deal provides the basis for a secure future for both companies and their employees.

The variants are innumerable – the trick is to decide the *essential* message, and to ensure that all future PR is consistent with that message.

When formulating this essential message it is useful to give some thought to the ideal headline you would like to see when the deal is announced. It is highly unlikely that the media will oblige, but going through the exercise will help you form the essential message – and perhaps to modify it. For instance, you may wish your employees to be reassured with a headline such as 'Jobs ensured by company X deal'. Or you may not welcome a headline like this, which may not assist the possible need for rationalisation. You may look for a headline aimed at your competitors, e.g. 'Company X deal strengthens market position', or at your shareholders, e.g. 'Company X deal consolidates earnings potential', etc.

Thinking about the basic message from a very early stage will provide a reference point throughout the negotiation stage. As negotiations proceed, it may need to be modified. For instance, it might not prove possible to acquire the whole of company Y, but only some of its operations. The essential message, once written down, provides a sheet anchor for the deal against which many other aspects can be tested. It will eventually become your public 'core statement', but at this stage it is a vital *internal* discipline.

The three phases of PR

In any successful company takeover there are three distinct phases, though their duration and importance may vary enormously from deal to deal.

They are:

1. the negotiation stage,
2. the announcement of the deal,
3. follow-up after the announcement.

They are all important from a PR point of view. They need different handling, but equally they need to be consistent – hence the stress on the essential message/core statement. Some suggestions for handling each phase are offered below.

The negotiation stage

Leaving aside the internal PR preparation, what are you going to say to the outside world? The best and safest answer is *nothing!* To say anything is to risk inviting further searching questions, which may become increasingly difficult to cope with. A skilled journalist may well give the impression that most of the details of the deal are known, and is merely seeking your confirmation. Say nothing! The journalist may simply be fishing on the basis of a vague rumour. The best line is: 'Our policy is never to comment on market speculation', or something similar.

The 'we never comment' line may not be easy to sustain. There may be an actual leak of information, either from within your own company or from company Y. You may not know where the leak has occurred, and it will probably be a waste of time trying to trace it. If firm information is leaked, the media will publish it whatever you say; but if you stick rigorously to your 'no comment' line, you may not only avoid answering follow-up questions, but you remain consistent.

Two specific difficulties can arise. The first is the stance of company Y. If yours is a friendly, unopposed bid, it should be possible for both companies to adopt the 'we never comment' line. If, however, you are involved in a hostile bid, life becomes much more complicated (of which more later).

The second potentially serious problem is the reaction of your own employees to the leak. They (or their elected representatives) may express concern and demand to know the facts. Much will depend on your established systems for consultation, but basically you should aim to reassure them that they will be the first to hear as soon as there is something to hear. Any other approach is likely to compound the difficulties, and indeed may cause you to run foul of Stock Exchange regulations. (See Chapter 6 on legal aspects.)

At a later stage, it will be necessary to consider your different audiences – the media, the City, your own employees, and interested parties in the communities where you are located – but at this stage of the negotiation this should not be necessary. The message to all is: 'We do not comment on speculation'.

The announcement of the deal

The correct handling of the actual announcement is obviously vital, but in order to get this right there is an equally important stage, which might be termed the 'run-up' to the announcement.

The run-up stage can be very short or quite extended – days or weeks. It covers the period between believing that the deal will be made and signing a firm agreement – rather like buying a house and agreeing 'subject to contract'. As we all know, much can go wrong in this critical period. Who knows, you may be gazumped by another bidder, the vendor may take the 'property' off the market, and so on. Nevertheless, this is the period when your PR preparation should be at its most intense. If the deal falls through the effort will be wasted; but if it goes ahead, careful preparation at this stage will pay off handsomely.

There are many ways to tackle your preparations. The approach suggested below is somewhat mechanistic, but it is tried and tested!

First, set out your *essential message* in writing and keep it in front of you throughout the process. At every subsequent stage, test what you have produced against that message. You may be surprised at the contradictions which arise.

Secondly, consider your audiences and their particular interests. Depending on the size and nature of the deal, they may include the following groups, with interests broadly as indicated:

The City

If you are a quoted company, the City will clearly be vitally interested, whether you are buying for cash or with 'paper', i.e. a share offer/share swap or some combination of cash and shares.

What will the City want to know? Above all, they will be interested in the effect of the deal on your share price and on the future prospects of your company. Hence, once again, the importance of the key message. But apart from this central interest, they will have a lot of other questions to ask. For instance, what have you paid for company Y? Are you going to tell them? Do you *have* to tell them under Stock Exchange rules? How are you going to finance the deal? Will it stretch your short-term position by increasing your borrowings? If so, what is likely to be the 'payback' period before your borrowing is back?

Your employees and the employees of company Y

The prime interest of both groups of employees will inevitably revolve around job security/redundancies and future prospects. Once again, the key message is vital. Is the rationale for the deal based on cost-cutting, including jobs? If so, which jobs and in which company? One or both? Or will there be no job losses?

It is fairly rare in any acquisition to be able to promise without reservation that the acquisition will result in *more* jobs, at least in the short term. Employees, particularly those in company Y, are likely to be worried and suspicious. Will their wage rates be maintained? Are their pension arrangements safe, or will they have to accept worse conditions? These are fair questions which deserve an answer. If by careful preparation you are able to satisfy them, the employees are far and away your best PR ambassadors. If you fail, no amount of PR will counter their legitimate concerns.

The local community

The interest of local parties will depend on the size and importance of the deal in the area concerned. Nevertheless, it is important to have local interests on your side. They will probably include the local MPs, not only the constituency MP, but also those in adjacent constituencies in which the workforce may live – the so-called travel-to-work areas.

The concern of these MPs are the same as the employees' – job security/employment prospects, etc. Lost jobs may mean lost votes!

The local authorities may have wider interests, relating to the impact on local services, planning issues, etc. For example, are you taking over the local bus company in order to close it down and eliminate competition? Are you buying the local gravelpits in the hope of extending quarrying operations? Or are you buying company Y in order to get your hands on its local property/land assets, which you then intend to put to some other use which may be unwelcome to local residents?

The media

Finally, the interests of the press in all its forms – national press (financial and non-financial), television and radio (national and local), local newspapers, and so on.

Again, the size and scope of the deal will obviously determine the level of interest. But there is a common thread, namely that journalists are looking for 'a story'. So back once again to the key message and the question: 'What headline would I like to see?'

The message to the media will be contained in your press release (of which more shortly). But if you have carefully considered your other audiences you will be in a very good position to handle the media's enquiries.

Ideally, it is worth planning the PR preparation systematically, rather like a military operation, on the days running up to the announcement itself. Think of announcement day as 'D Day'. Then plan for 'D Day minus four, three, two, one'. What do you need to have ready several days ahead? At what stage can you draft your press release? When can you compare notes on phraseology with your opposite numbers in company Y? What kind of statement are you going to make to your staff? Who is going to communicate with the staff of company Y? How do you pull all the messages together to ensure that they are consistent?

The idea of a well-planned programme is very enticing. However, at least two timing problems can arise which may make it extremely difficult to define 'D Day'. First, the negotiation itself. Even assuming a friendly, agreed bid, there are a host of legal and financial details to be agreed before signing, quite apart from the usually thorny problem of the price for the deal. Secondly, from a PR standpoint, there are obviously good and bad days for announcing the deal, depending on your desire for media coverage. Mid-week is clearly best if you wish to achieve maximum coverage. If, on the other hand, you are for good reasons seeking minimum exposure, late on Friday is probably the best time! You may, however, be constrained in your choice. Depending on the size and nature of the deal, Stock Exchange rules may demand that you announce at the earliest possible time after agreement has been reached. For instance, you may reach agreement in the early hours of the morning. If so, you may be required to announce the deal as soon as the Stock Exchange opens. If, moreover, you are acquiring an overseas company, in a different time zone, you will have to consider how you line up your local Stock Exchange requirements with those of the overseas Stock Exchange, be it New York, Tokyo or Frankfurt.

If you succeed in finding your way through this maze of time difference and legal requirements, you can then define 'D Day', i.e. the day on which news of your acquisition breaks. You are now in a position to work back from that day and plan ahead for the ultimate announcement.

Where should you start? Again, with the key statement, i.e. the reason for acquiring company Y – which you have written down, of course

The next step is to write down *all* the questions which may be asked, and to marshal them into some reasonable order, having regard to your various audiences. You will probably need a set of questions (and eventual answers) for:

1. your employees,
2. the employees of company Y,
3. the City editors and analysts,
4. the media,
5. possibly the local community (Council/local MPs, etc.).

The question-and-answer preparation is tedious but well worthwhile. You will, if you are assiduous, think of dozens of questions which, in the event, are not asked, but the discipline is invaluable. By the time you come to face live questions, you will be very well prepared. And despite your careful preparatory work, you will inevitably still get the 'sidewinder' question which occurred to no one!

The next recommended mechanistic stage is for those primarily concerned – your chief executive, financial, personnel and PR people and, above all, your selected spokesperson – to test the questions – and more particularly the answers – against your core statement. Is everything consistent? Are you presenting a coherent story? You will be surprised at the inconsistencies which can easily creep in at this crucial stage.

Having tested your questions and answers, it is worth sorting them into 'audiences', e.g. your staff, company Y's staff, the City, the media, and so on. Then your appropriate spokespeople for the different audiences will be able to have their own tailor-made set of papers from which to work.

Now comes the press release. After all, the questions and answers are there to answer questions from others; but you have the opportunity to get your own message across *before* anyone has the opportunity to ask any questions. The press release is your scene-setter.

Some journalists are lazy – they like to have their work done for them. They may therefore simply print your own press release in whole or in part. Even more assiduous journalists will probably use some of your own words. In particular, all journalists like a direct quote. In preparing your press release, therefore, first think back to your key message or core statement and build this into the title, e.g:

'Company X consolidates US market position.'
'Company X strengthens its research resource.'

If you include a quote, it should be short and pithy, and again should reflect your key message. Ideally, it should be attributed to the chairman or chief executive. If his opposite number in company Y is also prepared to be quoted in a supportive, positive manner, this will obviously be a bonus. Headlines indicating 'a good deal for both companies' might then be achieved, and that is probably the best of all worlds.

Bearing in mind the need to help the busy journalist, it is useful to keep the press release to the essentials, and not to load it with lots of technical information on products, or with financial background other than the figures required by the Stock Exchange, or to ensure accurate interpretation by City journalists and analysts. Detailed data, which may be welcome to specialist journalists and others with a specific interest in the deal, can be attached to the press release as 'Notes for Editors'.

The package of information described, i.e. the core statement, press release, message for employees and the questions and answers, can be prepared some time ahead of 'D Day' for announcement of the deal. It should certainly be available at the latest by, say, 'D Day minus three', because thereafter the pace of final negotiations is likely to take precedence.

The problems of preparing the PR package in advance are two-fold. First, there is the need for confidentiality; and secondly, some of the data, e.g. the final price, will not be available until the last moment. In this electronic age, however, these problems are not insurmountable. The paperwork can usually be prepared on word processors, whose operators do not need to have the most sensitive details until they slot them in at the last moment, thereby avoiding the risk of breaching Stock Exchange Rules and of possible premature leaks.

And so to D Day – the climax, or often the anti-climax of perhaps months of negotiation. How are you going to play it? Is it to be a 'big bang' or a low-key affair? It is probable that you will want to celebrate the 'marriage' of companies X and Y. Marriages call for celebrations to which you invite your friends – in this case your key audiences – so that they may celebrate with you. If, on the other hand, you are involved in a fiercely contested bid, you will be seeking to convince the interested parties that you have done what was needed by the other party – but it may not be an occasion for celebration!

Announcement day

Let us assume that we have a marriage and celebration. Look at the 'wedding guest list'. It will include the audiences already defined, i.e. the employees of companies X and Y, the City, possibly the local community, and certainly the media. Rather like a wedding, you have to decide who will come to the church, who will be invited to the reception, and who will come to the disco afterwards. A silly analogy? Not really. Just as with a wedding arrangement it is important not to give offence. It is very important to get matters in the right order.

First and foremost, if you are a quoted company, the 'banns' have to be read at the Stock Exchange. You ignore these at your peril. Indeed if you do, they are likely to find just cause why the 'union' may not go ahead. You cannot read the banns in advance, but you must ensure that the Stock Exchange is the first to know of your intentions. Hence the timing of your Stock Exchange announcement sets the scene for the rest of the day.

This does not mean that you cannot *simultaneously* (or thereabouts) inform your employees or their elected representatives, and it is wise to do so. In an ideal world, therefore, you may be able to announce the deal to the Stock Exchange soon after it is open for business on announcement day, leaving the rest of the day clear for your other audiences. Announcing to the Stock Exchange will probably entail sending them copies of your press release, provided it contains the essential information required under the rules. You may choose either to deliver copies or to transmit the information electronically if you have the facility.

What next? Again, much depends on the size of the deal, and its importance to your share price. In a major deal, it is worth considering a conference for City analysts and/or journalists. They do not like to be invited together; and there are good reasons for this. First, their interests – and hence their questions – are somewhat different. Secondly, their timescales and deadlines on the day are also different. Analysts need the opportunity of questioning you ahead of journalists. Moreover, journalists, after questioning you, are likely to seek a second opinion from the expert analysts. Hence there is much to be said for seeing analysts first, followed closely by the media.

If the deal is sufficiently important, it is likely, as indicated, that you will wish to organise conferences for analysts, followed by journalists. If so, it is worth considering a rehearsal (if time permits) of your key spokespeople. The main question to decide is 'Who is going to speak to what?' Do not have too many spokespeople, otherwise you can guarantee that they will begin to contradict each other and give the questioners a field day.

Consider handouts to help those attending: obviously the press release, but perhaps back-up material on the product range, photographs of the production plants, or whatever. Perhaps even consider a celebratory drink afterwards, but remember that you are dealing with a basically cynical, or at best a questioning, audience who are unlikely to be impressed by any attempt at the hard sell. They have come to get hard facts, not propaganda.

For the small deal, it may be adequate to issue press releases and other printed material to analysts and journalists, together with names/telephone numbers of appointed contacts. None the less, it is still important to appoint key spokespeople, and to ensure that they are adequately provided with working documents, questions and answers, etc.

The aftermath of the announcement

The initial proof of the pudding, i.e. whether the PR handling of the announcement was good, will be most apparent on the following day. First, the media coverage. Collect it, read it carefully and retain it. Do not be put off by the headlines. They matter, but they are written by sub-editors not by the journalists who came to your conference. The text matters more than the headlines – those who really matter to you will read the text.

The next test, if you are a quoted company, will be the reaction of your share price in the City. Here again, it pays not to jump to instant conclusions. The City is a volatile institution. When it has had time to digest the details of the deal, its second thoughts may be quite different from its initial reaction. And in any event, there may be other powerful market forces at work on the day which completely overshadow the importance of the deal. So the key message is: 'Don't shoot your spokesperson on the day after the announcement!' Give him at least a few days' reprieve.

Even after the excitement of the announcement period, there is still a vital role for PR. The City analysts will continue to follow the deal's fortunes, as will your employees, the employees of company Y and all the other interested parties. What did you say about profit forecasts, about borrowing requirements, about job security or plant closures? Sweet words whispered before the wedding day are often quoted back after the event! Journalists in particular have long memories and very good information files.

It is vital, therefore, to store the PR data for a while, especially the key message/core statement and the questions and answers. If they were well prepared, they will be robust and stand the test of the months after the event. Remember the trowel analogy? If the trowelling work was good, the resulting edifice will not only look good, it will be waterproof (and hopefully fireproof as well!).

It would be wrong to give the impression that the aftermath period should be defensive from a PR standpoint. It may, if the acquisition fulfils its promise, provide the opportunity for further positive media coverage. If initial results of the acquired company are good, why not remind the City, the media and the employees? Given a skilful PR touch, you don't have to say 'We told you so'. With luck and a light touch, your audiences will come to that conclusion themselves.

The contested bid

The contested bid is not a subject for a few words in one chapter on PR, but worthy of a book in its own right.

Contested bids tend to be largely, though not exclusively, the domain of large public companies, possessing considerable in-house legal, personnel and PR resources. It is, moreover, an area where the merchant banks come into their own. In most such bids there is a scramble between the contending parties to retain the services of the 'best' merchant bank, and thereafter to rely heavily on their advice, on PR as well as other issues.

With that in mind, most of the foregoing advice on PR remains valid. The key message/core statement remains vital (and no merchant bank can write that for you though they may help). Your main audience in a contested situation consists of the shareholders of company Y. Will they vote for or against your offer? But the shareholders will inevitably be influenced by the analysts and the media. And your own shareholders and staff may also need convincing that the bid is in their own interests. So back to square one.

In a contested bid, the competition policy aspects are likely to attract the attention of the Office of Fair Trading or the Monopolies and Mergers Commission (or the competition authorities of the EEC). These are not subjects for this chapter, but they cannot be ignored from the PR standpoint, and your questions and answers will have to take these aspects into account.

In the most fiercely fought battles, the battlefield frequently becomes the media, with expensive full-page advertisements of charge and counter-charge between the parties. The rules governing such advertising are rigorous. No advertisement may mislead shareholders. Indeed, such advertisements require a statement of factual accuracy to be certified by the directors of the company. In such circumstances, the only sensible advice to give is take professional advice. Have any advertising checked by your merchant bank, your own financial people and your lawyers.

In the end, however, everything reverts to the key message. If this fails to convince the stakeholders of the soundness of the deal, the bid will almost certainly fail.

External PR advice

Some readers may be daunted by the recommendations in this chapter. Their reaction may be: 'That's fine for the big boys, but I haven't the time or the people to go through all this preparation.' Equally, there will be those who already have a well-ordered PR system who will glean little – though hopefully something – from the suggestions.

Those facing the most daunting PR task are likely to be the small/medium-sized companies for whom buying another company is the most attractive form of rapid growth, but for whom the handling of PR in such circumstances is a new experience. They may have little experience of dealing with the media, indeed they may not know the most important journalists or even how to handle the distribution of a press release – or how to write one! But all is not lost. There is a host of PR agencies, large and small, anxious to help – for a fee. That is no slur on PR agencies. From the largest to the smallest, they possess the necessary expertise to assist you but they naturally expect to be recompensed for their services.

Choosing an agency is difficult, but there are sources of information available, such as the Institute of Public Relations. Check the claims of a particular agency, especially the areas where they claim expertise, then ask for their client list. Next, as in taking on any other service, ask for references from some of their clients to ensure that they were satisfied with the service they received.

Having made a choice without commitment, discuss your needs with the agency. Having gone back through your checklist of actions, decide what you can and wish to do yourself, using your own resources. Then decide *precisely* the remit for the agency, i.e. what do you want them to do, and when and how do you want them to do it? Expect a little give-and-take, and don't ignore their arguments. After all, you are employing expertise which you lack.

Having reached that stage, agree the fee, the payment terms and the deadlines by which you expect specific services to be provided. Most relationships between PR agencies and clients fail because of ambiguity either on the precise brief or on the deadlines by which the agency was expected to come up with the goods.

Finally, get two competitive quotations!

Conclusion

Jonathan Swift said, 'Providence never intended to make the management of public affairs a mystery to be comprehended only by a few persons of sublime genius.' He might equally well have been describing the management of public relations. After all, PR is an integral part of public affairs management. All PR practitioners, like any other professionals, like to cloak their expertise in a degree of mystique. Their livelihood depends on it! And they are not entirely wrong to do so. If you need a lawyer, you do not call a doctor, and vice versa.

That said, the handling of public relations is a 50 : 50 mixture of common sense and technique. The common sense, in any acquisition, can only reside in the company making the takeover. They may lack the PR technique, in which case they are well advised to buy in expertise; but this chapter has sought to argue that bought-in expertise is no substitute for careful in-house preparation.

Much has been made of the need to rely on the key message or core statement. No apology is made for this. In the view of this author, it is the absolute key to success or failure.

If you can condense the key reason for the takeover to a couple of sentences, you will have produced a yardstick against which to measure all your subsequent actions and decisions. It cannot be emphasised too strongly that the value of the core statement exercise as a discipline is as much internal as external. The writer has known situations where concentration on this approach has actually caused company directors to rethink their strategy partially or totally.

Hence careful PR preparation is not only a tool, it is an integral part of a takeover plan. If well organised, it becomes the devil's advocate. It asks the questions: 'What if . . .?', 'How?', 'Why?', 'When?' And it compels those concerned to produce answers in advance of the event. It also forces different interests in the takeover company – the Board, the lawyers, the personnel function, the accountants, the planners – and not least the PR people themselves – to think as a *group*, rather than to concentrate on their narrower expert interests.

The techniques described may perhaps best be described as a game of Snakes and Ladders. Follow the plan, and half-way up the board you will come sliding down and have to start again. But if you persist, you will end up at the top, and announcement day will be that much easier.

But you'll still never think of that one sidewinder question!

Chapter 9

Post-acquisition management

RICHARD WOOD

Senior Business Manager, ICI

Introduction

This chapter brings together lessons and experiences from a range of acquisitions made primarily by the author and his company to highlight a number of key factors which will need to be addressed positively if implementation is to proceed smoothly and successfully.

Successful post-acquisition management begins long before the deal has been signed. In Kitching's (1973) study,[1] 40 per cent of the outcomes of acquisitions made were shown to be due to the implementation phase. Thus if the principal components of developing an acquisition strategy have been carried out efficiently, identifying the objectives, finding the right business and making a full investigation, the task will have been minimised. The greatest implementation challenge will then be the transitional management of staff.

A basic conclusion of Vivian's[2] work on the history of post-acquisition management was that when the managements of two separate businesses with different systems and styles are involved in a takeover or merger, a staggering range of unexpected difficulties surface in the post-acquisition period. Many of the difficulties have been shown to arise through omissions or unfulfilled promises made by key people in the pre-implementation phase which were either misplaced or misunderstood. If not carefully managed, such situations can lead to an irreversible set of quite destructive organisation dynamics.

Later sections of this chapter highlight how the communication processes can be managed to minimise potential organisation problems and personnel issues so that management attention can also be focused on the development and implementation of a post-acquisition plan in the way set out in the final section.

The pre-implementation phase

The extent of a candidate company's integration into an existing business, or the level of changes necessary, will depend on the reason for acquisition. It could lie anywhere between the extremes of full integration and operation as a stand-alone subsidiary. Sometimes the acquisition strategy will have required that vigorous action be taken after the purchase, perhaps to divest a part of the acquisition of non-strategic importance. In other cases major organisational changes or a change of scope will be necessary to meet new objectives.

All these factors will need to have been defined early on as they will inevitably impact on the deal as well as on the post-acquisition plan. Indeed, they represent the starting point for this plan and should cover all aspects of strategic, financial, operational and personnel management of the business. It must, in addition, take into account all the likely risks involved.

Even in the best managed acquisition negotiations, situations will require that certain decisions be made quickly and on the basis of limited information. On other occasions, concessions will have to be made to achieve an acceptable deal.

Such changes of scope, or intent, will undoubtedly have added to the risk and, although perhaps reflected in the price agreed for the purchase, they will not have altered the goals or expectations for the business when it moves into the post-acquisition phase. Also, pressures during negotiations will have left little time for the negotiators and the on-going business managers to communicate freely; it is likely that matters of short-term impact on business performance will have been given less consideration by the negotiators than those longer-term aspects, more important in making a good strategic deal. These factors point clearly to the necessity for some form of continuity or overlap between the management of the negotiation and the post-acquisition management. How this is achieved will depend on the organisational structure adopted for running the business and the relative skills of the individuals involved. Options include making a leading negotiator responsible for post-acquisition management, or giving the senior manager responsibility well ahead of the deal being struck and involving this manager in the final stages of drawing up agreements.

A final factor of significance is that while negotiations have been in progress, the candidate business will have been running itself, most of its senior managers being heavily involved either directly in the negotiations or indirectly in providing information and disclosures for them. Thus, some decisions likely to affect the immediate and medium-term business performance will have been made without the usual careful consideration. Other factors will have been neglected or postponed and may, by the time of the signing, have become of a critical nature. These as well as the temporary setback to business performance always apparent after a takeover, have been major causes of the failure of a number of acquisitions in the past and have been highlighted in several business school studies of the history of acquisitions.

The announcement

It is vitally important that all the staff of the new business know precisely the reason for the acquisition and the role their business will have in the organisation it is to join. For the majority of staff, the story will be interesting and positive, full of hope for a successful future – not a difficult message to communicate. However, there are many pitfalls particularly where enthusiasm leads to over-statement which may later be seen by the audience as partially-delivered firm promises. The subsequent disappointments lead to loss of credibility for the management.

To set against this risk, the taking of a wholly non-committal stance will of course destroy credibility before it has even had a chance to be established. There is therefore a tightrope that must be walked with care and critical attention. Vivian's (1988) study showed that in more than one half of the acquisitions rated successful a major factor, which the acquired management emphasised as contributing to an overall commitment to the new owner, was that assurances given were rigidly adhered to.

In most acquisition processes there will have been time during the detailed legal procedures to consult directors or senior managers in the candidate company about how best to make the initial communications and to address the likely concerns of the company's staff, suppliers and customers. Experience has shown that it is of immense help to prepare a package of information carefully matched to that of the press release but expanded to include answers to the specific concerns of each audience. Prepared sets of typical questions and answers can be supplied to various groups to structure discussion towards key points. These also assist the announcers at various locations to deal with problems and communications in a similar way.

An efficient communication process is of equal importance for the morale of the staff and the credibility of the new management. No one must learn about the deal from a newspaper or trade union representative before officially being told by the management.

Arrangements should be made for a two-way operation with an opportunity for employees to question points and explore concerns. This may entail a general mass meeting with limited opportunity for questions and follow-up sessions for managers to address smaller groups over a more extended timeframe.

The initial contact with customers and suppliers will be by letter, promptly followed by a visit or telephone call, to deal with misunderstandings, problems and concerns. The credibility of the new business in the marketplace is key to managing the likely downsides in short-term performance. It should be remembered that staff will be temporarily less effective for several weeks or even months after the takeover, often more concerned about themselves than the fate of the business.

During this period, the wrong impression can easily be given to the marketplace by what may seem to the management or staff to be reasonable comments about the uncertainty associated with the vast amount of change with which they are faced. For instance, a casual comment from the customer service desk like, 'it's all changing here and no one knows what's going to happen next', can quickly start adverse market rumours, lose customer confidence and ultimately market share to the competition.

Post-acquisition managerial control

There are three basic justifications for having bought the business:

1. profitability,
2. growth, organic or diversification,
3. control of risk.

3 BASIC JUSTIFICATIONS FOR BUYING A BUSINESS.

No matter which has been the case, the principal task for immediate post-acquisition action will be to gain a firm control of:

1. profit,
2. growth,
3. risk,
4. liquidity,
5. corporate image, and
6. job satisfaction.

In addition, it is important to set delegated authority levels so that all managers will understand their powers and responsibilities for running a 'tight ship'.

To control profitability and liquidity, or even more general performance against business targets, a precise, short-term action plan must be implemented immediately. If there has been the recommended overlap between the negotiators and the business managers, there will have been less difficulty in drawing one up.

In any event, it is a team task involving all the senior managers in the business. It will also provide a useful forum in which to judge the acquired business manager's relative strengths and weaknesses and their grasp not only of departmental activity but also their ability to contribute to the management of the business as a whole.

Where growth is to be pursued through the acquisition, it is not enough to create the potential for that growth. The business must be positively positioned to achieve it and careful thought must be given to identifying realistic short-term actions for implementing the changes necessary.

Where synergies are being sought or the company merged into the parent, the problems are different. Managements are likely to overlap significantly, there will be considerable levels of redundancy to manage and, if the best of both organisations is to be retained, there will be disappointed people in both the acquired and parent companies.

It is often the case that changes of this nature are usually encouraged to evolve over an extended period with several consultation steps to discover what is the best structure for the business. However, when the pattern of aims for the business is changed as significantly as during a merger, it becomes critical that the aims are achieved as quickly as possible. This will minimise the uncertainty which lowers morale and misdirects people's efforts into self-preservation rather than furthering the business needs.

If it has been decided to leave the initial management intact, it will be a mistake to assume that they will understand fully the intentions and priorities of the new parent. Left alone, they are most likely to perform as in the past. It is thus essential from the outset to have at least 'an eyes and ears' person seconded to the business. This may be a commercial person, but is more likely to be an accountant with a general business experience. If the existing CEO is not an especially strong personality and is likely to get bogged down with compromise solutions, it would be worthwhile seconding a new CEO. This is more likely to be successful than telling the existing CEO to change as well as the company.

The honeymoon period

Immediately following the acquisition, if the announcements have gone well and any redundancies have been handled skilfully, the business will enter a honeymoon period. Morale will initially be high as people not made redundant will be pleased to have a job and they may assume that the new owners have answers to the problems previously encountered by the business. The biggest mistake is to think that this initial euphoria will be long-lasting and that managers can concentrate on the many pressing business tasks with few continuing personnel issues. History has shown that this will not be so. The honeymoon period will be short-lived and, within months, sometimes weeks, managers may find they are wrestling with severe personnel problems.

[handwritten margin note: Poor Comm + few job assurance]

If honest and convincing assurances about the future of the business
cannot be provided, and it seems likely that only limited progress can be
made to resolve problems as the staff see them, key employees will simply *[handwritten: turnover]*
look elsewhere. With mature reflection, well-established employees who
have survived the takeover often analyse the situation thus: 'Things aren't
improving! My colleague who lived for the company was made redundant,
so I had better leave now before I'm pushed.'

There are four golden rules of managerial style in handling staff during *[handwritten: How you treat redundant staff affects those kept on]*
this transitional period:

1. Be generous with former employees' redundancy terms and let the
    remaining staff know about it.
2. Convince remaining staff that any cuts in numbers or changes to
    the cost structure are a last resort. This will mean sharing with them
    parts of the financial reasoning behind the decision.
3. Keep open communication lines and deal with problems and worries
    quickly to inspire confidence in the new management and in its ability
    to develop the business and resolve difficulties.
4. Be honest.

Communications

An efficient and effective two-way communication structure using line
managers should be set up. It should be used initially to disseminate
the new business philosophies and objectives, detailed commercial and
operational objectives, as well as some aspects of financial performance
and personnel policies and style. It should offer opportunities for staff
to probe for understanding, to vent concerns and bring forward
suggestions.

This communication structure will then be used to refine and implement
the post-acquisition management plan. It will also be used to deal with any
ongoing concerns and with the ideas of staff, so building the credibility
of the management team.

Communication style should be straightforward about bad news.
Looming problems should be exposed. There is only one thing worse
than bad news and that is uncertainty. Also, employees should be given
the chance to vent their feelings and mourn unpalatable changes before
they are pressed to settle down and make them work.

In communicating with the parent, senior managers must be given the
opportunity to bring forward their own concerns and the worries and
problems of staff and most importantly, ideas for developing the business
and meeting business goals.

The post-acquisition management plan

The business

After a takeover, the acquired management is looking for a clear vision of the broad directions in which the new owners wish the company to develop. They also want to know the new management's business philosophy and intended actions. In many instances it has been found helpful to develop a mission statement for the business and to use it to lead discussion into the setting of a detailed list of business objectives to be used as the basis for a new corporate plan. These objectives should cover all the normal business parameters, but should emphasise:

1. research,
2. commercial targets,
3. financial control,
4. production targets,
5. personnel policy,
6. management style.

This first corporate plan should be top-down in nature and of an appropriate duration for the type of business. For example, in the case of businesses heavily dependent on research, the timeframe will need to be several years whilst for other businesses a one to two-year plan will be adequate. Because time is of the essence, it should be developed by the senior managers with only limited consultation with their staff. After full communication to the staff it should be used with greater consultation to develop new departmental budgets as it is unlikely under the new plan that the old budgets will remain valid for more than a few months.

The overall process is lengthy and time-consuming but it has been found to be critical in the development of a new culture and direction for the acquired business as well as a sound understanding of departments and key individuals' accountability in the new organisational structure.

Organisational structure

It is likely that changes to the Board or senior management structure will have been announced at the time of the acquisition. A second-phase communication should thus be planned to include the evolution of the structure into the lower levels of the organisation. This phase will need to commence with the redefinition of the role of major departments and work groups to demonstrate how they will fit into the new structure and how they will be expected to contribute to achieving the business goals.

In this more detailed phase, every effort should be made to evolve the structure with the full commitment of the staff. Without their involvement, experience has shown that staff will see the changes either as change for the sake of change or panacea for solving past problems, which if not solved, memories will recall the good old days for which miraculously the problems will have been evaporated. As a result there will be no incentive to make the new structure work and there will be a loss of confidence in the management.

Personnel policy and management style

In all established businesses, historical anomalies will have crept into the pay and conditions structure. The introduction of sweeping operational and organisational changes associated with the acquisition offer a golden opportunity to start afresh and to design new policies to meet the future business needs. Indeed, certain promises may have already been given to the staff or the previous owners in order to gain support for the acquisition deal. Often this may have included statements about increased levels of remuneration in the future.

However, even if such promises have not been made, experience has shown that staff of acquired businesses expect their remuneration packages to be improved. Even in historically unprofitable businesses, the staff have a common expectation that the new owners, seen to be the rescuers, will improve their terms and conditions. This may seem to be unrealistic and unreasonable but it is nevertheless the case. One must remember that in businesses with an unprofitable history, staff salary increases will have been held back over several years and there will have been an undercurrent feeling that pay levels had been eroded below that of the competition even if this is not the case.

Erosion may well have occurred in middle and junior managers' and clerical workers' packages although it is less likely for senior management who, smaller in number and generally more mobile, will have been able to negotiate individually competitive packages, if they are key to the future of the business. Also shopfloor workers, if represented by a union, will usually have managed to at least keep wage increases abreast of inflation.

The new management must thus plan to address this problem and to build its cost into the business plan. In deciding the level of cost it should be remembered that people's minds will generally concentrate more on the anomalies between themselves and their colleagues than on national comparisons. Therein lies the key to achieving a harmonious transition.

A process that has been used with success is to employ an independent consultant to carry out a comparative study of terms and conditions in companies of a similar size and type in the industry. This report can then be used as background to make a corporate statement on average pay levels, for instance 'we will be paying the median level for the industry', and to demonstrate if it is the case, that remuneration has only fallen behind in certain areas.

Anomalies can be corrected by the use of a job evaluation process which will regrade all the jobs within the new organisational structure. Although this sounds like a mammoth task, it is not really. Experienced assessors will be able to highlight the benchmark jobs and anomalies which can be assessed within a few months. Other jobs will then follow over an extended period. The result will be to take the heat out of any immediate feelings of injustice and to make a positive demonstration that, in future, general adjustments to pay will keep pace with the industry norm.

An area not often dealt with during the acquisition negotiations because of its complexity and the length of time it takes actuaries to do their work, is pensions. It has been found helpful to set up a pension working party of staff and management trustees under the guidance of the actuaries to report on pensions. However, it is unlikely that such a report will be completed or implemented within the first year of operation of the business and so temporary pension arrangements will need to have been made (see Chapter 7).

The foregoing suggestions for handling pay and conditions and the communication process outlined in the previous section, are clearly important components of a management style found to be effective. The acquired management knows the new owner has potential for exercising considerable power for changing the business and they virtually expect the buyer to use that power. If the new owner does not address these expectations by communicating a clear vision of the future, fear of uncertainty about 'what's he up to' will increase.

No matter what new management style is adopted, it is unlikely to be the same as the one used by the previous management and will thus need to be communicated well if it is to be understood by the staff and acted upon in a homogeneous way by the management team. In adopting any new style, care should be taken not to make such major changes, that the effect on the normal working environment is to remove the essential shape of the company and to divert attention from the main task of improving the business.

Financial control

A strong financial function is a critical component for the success of the post-acquisition management phase. If the parent company has seconded a senior financial person to the organisation this person will at least be able to communicate the level and style of reporting to the parent company and to help the management team to understand what the new parent believes to be the important ratios and factors for progressing the business. If no one has been seconded, it will be important for the existing controller to make an immediate visit to HQ to ascertain this detail.

Reporting to the new parent may be very demanding for small businesses simultaneously wrestling with post-acquisition changes. In the short term, some of the options open are to second a lower-level accountant from HQ to help or to employ one of the company's auditors at consolidation time.

From the outset, the new and strengthened financial function must provide the members of the Board or management team with a timely financial service of management accounts covering sales, profitability and cashflow, sufficiently accurate to enable business decisions to be made. Well-presented historical figures will be of theoretical interest only.

The first task for the controller will be to prepare a status report on the business performance to date as the closure of the acquisition is likely to have been based on an historic set of accounts with the current position only being estimated. This status report should be the basis of a debate with the management team on the prognosis for the remaining months of the year and used as the starting point for the high level management account based plan mentioned above for use in progressing and monitoring the business during this period. It may also highlight information which indicates that disclosures by the previous owners have not been comprehensive and that a warranty claim is possible (see Chapter 6).

Detailed effort should then be directed at producing the budget for the following year and any other years in the normal budgeting cycle, based on the new objectives for the business.

The budget forecasts should be prepared in consultation with line managers based on a simple financial picture agreed with the Board and the parent company. Ideally, they should be formulated on a product and market basis and operating costs and fixed expenses should be broken down in a detailed chart of accounts under appropriate cost centres so that careful control can be effected and clear accountability given to line managers.

Research and development

While the new owners and the management team are heavily involved in the organisational and administrative changes of the acquisition, the research and development team are quite likely to believe that they are or will possibly become a 'Cinderella organisation'. This situation will be amplified if, as a result of the budget process or the short-term position of the business, cuts have to be made to research expenditure in order to trim costs and achieve profit forecasts. It is thus critical for the long-term future of the business and to retain senior scientific staff, that shortcuts in the communication process are not taken and R & D staff are kept fully involved. If the management style suggested in this chapter is adopted, the R & D team will have been involved in the initial communications, the standard communication and response systems, the formulation of research objectives, the introduction to the personnel policy and management style debate and finally, in the budgetary control process. In total, this should minimise any potential problems but it is an area which should be carefully monitored.

Sales and marketing

In most small and medium-sized companies the sales force is the work group with the most volatile level of morale. Seemingly minor successes or setbacks oscillate them between euphoria and doom. It is therefore necessary to stabilise morale in the sales force at an early stage so that there will be a minimum of disruption to the effort placed on progressing the business in the delicate stages immediately following acquisition.

It is quite likely that the new owners will have conceptualised that there should be a relaunch of the company image and many of its main product lines at some stage. The answer is to do it earlier rather than later. Such a relaunch will often be entrusted to an outside agency to develop so it need not conflict with the time pressures of the other organisational work being undertaken by the management team. Indeed, it is a good plan to brief the agency to be involved as soon as possible after the announcement of the acquisition or indeed before then, even involving the agency in the press and other communication processes of the acquisition itself. This will provide useful background for the agency and cut out one stage of briefing.

Having told the sales force that a relaunch is being planned, the involvement of the senior sales staff and the marketing staff at strategic points in its development, will provide sufficient feedback to keep sales force interest maintained and morale high in the expectation of things to come. The relaunch of the corporate image can then be planned at a convenient time in the business cycle, but should normally be targeted well within six months after the acquisition date if it is to have the full effect.

Production

If the trade unions representing the workforces have been appropriately involved and carefully managed during the latter stages of the acquisition process, there should be no greater problems in developing a harmonious working relationship with them and the workforce than there were prior to the takeover. The sales force relaunch of the company image can usefully provide a vehicle upon which to begin an efficiency and productivity drive and to stimulate teamwork, particularly necessary where there have been major changes in manning levels and enforced changes to working practices.

Conclusion

No matter how long the decision and negotiation period of any acquisition, the task of post-acquisition management will take longer. Where a business must be turned around quickly, immediate actions will be necessary. This will be followed by a lengthy process of consolidation to produce a robust business organisation for the future. If a more passive approach is possible, perhaps because the acquisition was made just as an investment, it will still need close monitoring and managing.

Although no two acquisitions are alike, all have one thing in common, none will pass through the post-acquisition phase without some unexpected problems being encountered. The challenges of post-acquisition management are large, diverse and highly rewarding. For the management team involved, it should be more than just work, it should be fun – so enjoy it!

References

1. Kitching, J. (1973) *Acquisitions in Europe, Causes of Corporate Successes and Failures* (Business International SA).
2. Vivian, P. (1988) *Post Acquisition Management. The Human Factor.* Conference on How to Buy and Sell Private Companies.

Chapter 10

Minimising the risk factor in acquisitions

(handwritten margin note: CLASSIFICATI ACQUISITIONS 3 MAIN CATEGORIES)

THOMAS R. ANGEAR
Managing Director, Trabel Associates and M & A International

(handwritten margin note: STATS ON SUCCESS; at best only 50%.)

The previous chapters in this book have concentrated on the *mechanics* of a corporate acquisition strategy – the nuts and bolts of how to identify, evaluate, negotiate and successfully manage companies acquired as part of a deliberate policy of diversification. Yet, when all is said and done, acquisitions are still a relatively high-risk activity compared to other less glamorous avenues of corporate growth. Over the last twenty years or so a constant stream of research studies on both sides of the Atlantic has demonstrated beyond all reasonable doubt that, *at best*, only 50 per cent of acquisitions are ultimately judged to be successful. Assessments range from 'highly successful' to 'downright disastrous' and the message is unequivocal – there are no guaranteed recipes for success in this business. Given the well-documented nature of this high-profile activity over the last two decades what distinguishes the successes from the failures and what lessons can be learned regarding the pitfalls in pre-acquisition strategy and post-acquisition planning?

Horizontal, vertical and conglomerate acquisitions

(handwritten margin note: sticking to the knitting)

The overwhelming conclusion to be drawn from a wide range of studies initiated by John Kitching in 1967[1] and culminating in Professor Michael Porter's study in 1987[2] is that: *'The further one diversifies away from one's own industry in terms of production, customers or technology, the less successful one is likely to be.'*

The evidence is so universal that the statement should be regarded almost as a fundamental law of acquisitions. The theorem is endorsed by Peters and Waterman[3] who observed that excellent, innovative companies, *inter alia*, 'stick to the knitting'. Their observation drew heavily on the research of Richard Rumelt[4] who found that those businesses with '*dominant-constrained*' and '*related-constrained*' diversification strategies were unquestionably the best performers. Both these strategies were based upon the concept of *controlled diversity*. Rumelt explained that 'These companies have strategies of entering only those businesses that build on, draw strength from, and enlarge some central strength or competence. While such firms frequently develop new products and enter new businesses, they are loath to invest in areas that are unfamiliar to management.' He added that the better performing firms 'built their diversification strategies on some central skill or strength'. Rumelt based his analysis on the performance of a broad sample of Fortune 500 companies spread over a twenty-year period.

Acquisitions can be classified into three main categories:

1. *Horizontal acquisitions*, i.e. within the same industry where there are similarities in products, customers, suppliers and technology.
2. *Vertical acquisitions*, i.e. also within the same industry but where the customers or suppliers are different.
3. *Conglomerate acquisitions* in unrelated industries where there is no commonality of products, customers or technology.

The available evidence suggests that, on balance, horizontal acquisitions are likely to be more successful than vertical acquisitions and that both are likely to be more rewarding than conglomerate acquisitions. By way of example, a computer software company is likely to be more successful in purchasing another software house ('horizontal') than if it were to buy a retailer of computer systems ('vertical'). Although both targets are within the same computer services industry the buyer is likely to be more successful in the first case because the particular problems of software development costs, lead times, program 'bugs', etc. will be familiar. A move into retailing, however, would bring new problems of hardware maintenance, volume discount structures, customer training and credit control which could easily trap the inexperienced. Were this software house to contemplate a move into a totally unrelated industry, e.g. book publishing ('conglomerate') the consequences could be extremely painful.

Geographical and psychological distance

A less well-documented finding which is tabled here purely as a hypothesis is as follows:

The greater the geographical and psychological distance separating the buyer from the seller the *greater* the incidence of failure.

Most of the published evidence on *geographical distance* relates to exporting rather than acquisitions but the parallels are obvious. Johanson and Vahlne[5] developed the related concept of 'psychological distance' – geography, language, culture, social and technical distance, etc. – and it is clear that companies tend to make international acquisitions initially in those countries with the *lowest* psychological distance. It is by no means accidental that two of the most publicised acquisition failures in recent years – Midland Bank's purchase of Crocker National Bank in California and Imperial Group's experience with Howard Johnson – were both adventures into uncharted territory; the markets were unfamiliar and a long way from home. Were a prospective purchaser to make both cardinal errors at the same time – buying into a new business area in a foreign country – the chances of success are likely to be minimal.

In recent years, a number of small to medium-sized companies have made 'one-off' acquisitions in the USA with a purchase price of around $5–6 million. The strategy behind such moves is barely defensible. In the first place, a company of this size in the USA is likely to have only a small market share in its immediate locality and a negligible share in state (let alone national) markets. It could easily be put out of business by an aggressive competitor. More importantly, a company of this size is unlikely to have any depth of management talent and it is both impractical and very expensive to attempt to run a US operation from a British head office. One suspects that acquisitions of this nature will show a high casualty rate in future years.

Common acquisition mistakes

At a recent international conference the chief executive of a success-ful highly acquisitive British company made the following revealing statement: 'We could have paid significantly *more* for our successful acquisitions and they would still have been good. We could have paid significantly *less* for our unsuccessful acquisitions and they would still have been bad!'

Unsuccessful acquisitions can, in very general terms, be grouped into two main categories:

1. paying too much for the *wrong* company,
2. paying too much for the right company and failing to manage the business to *add value*.

The second category of failures would appear to be less common in practice. After all, if you buy the wrong company to begin with you should not expect your managers to perform post-acquisition miracles. The subject of post-acquisition management has been covered in detail in Chapter 9 and it is unnecessary to go over this ground again. However, it must be stated that if this aspect is badly handled, all the time and effort put into the investigation and negotiation phases will be totally destroyed. The key factor here would appear to be the *quality of management* on both sides of the equation.

Category 1 failures are the real problem children. How do professionally-managed companies get themselves into such a mess by buying the 'wrong' companies? Professor Michael Porter examined the diversification record of 33 large US companies from 1950 to 1986 and identified *three* main errors of judgement:

They spend too much money simply because they get into bidding wars. Or they rationalise rather than analyse the attractions of an industry. Or they fail to demonstrate to themselves how a proposed venture would enhance their overall corporate strategy.

It is easy to be carried away by a company auction. The fear of allowing a target company to fall into the hands of a direct competitor is a powerful argument in raising price thresholds. It should be remembered, however, that many successful companies are noted as much for the deals they 'don't do' as for the deals that they 'do'. Successful acquirers know when to say 'no' and have learned the art of walking away from a deal when the stakes get too high. This is not an easy art to master particularly when all the emotional and commercial momentum is in the opposite direction. US investment banks have become very skilled at the business of auctioning divisions of larger companies for the highest possible price by playing off one buyer against another. It is all too easy to get caught up with this merry-go-round.

Porter's study suggests that companies fall into *two* main traps of their own making:

1. They have a vague belief that the new business would 'fit in', but fail to recognise fundamentally weak industry structures.
2. They buy something because it appears cheap or simply because it is available for sale.

In addition, there is a tendency for ambitious diversifying companies to rush into embryonic industries, e.g. personal computers, confusing early, exponential growth with long-term profit potential.

Porter argues that one of the keys to making good acquisitions is *to find undervalued companies with good middle management*. Hanson, BTR, Williams Holdings and Tomkins are all successful exponents of this strategy. Their approach, however, is part of a deliberate corporate restructuring strategy followed by the rapid sell-off of subsidiaries which appear incapable of further improvement.

Acquisition errors in the USA

The author's first-hand experience of acquisitions by European companies in the USA suggest that the most common reasons for failure to meet expected performance are:

1. *Poor preparation,* in terms of strategic analysis of the benefits of the acquisition and the type of acquisition sought.
2. *Poor assessment* of the acquisition target's real earnings and growth potential.
3. *Poor market competitive analysis* shown in particular through:

    (a) underestimating the pace and nature of change in US markets,
    (b) overestimating the similarities between US and European markets,
    (c) underestimating the regional differences within the United States.

4. Adopting an inappropriate management style.

Foreign acquirers would improve their chances of success in the USA if they were prepared to spend as much time and effort on *market analysis* as they do on 'due diligence' investigations of the company in question.

The concept of relatedness

A parallel study to Michael Porter's work examined the 'value creation performance' of the acquisition programmes of 116 large US companies and came to very similar conclusions. Carried out by McKinsey and Co.,[6] the benchmark of success was a company's ability at least to earn back its cost of capital on the funds invested in its acquisition programme. On this measure, over 60 per cent of all the acquisitions were rated as failures with *large, unrelated takeovers* by far the most risky category with a failure rate of 86 per cent.

McKinsey advised that predators can make *three* cardinal errors which prevent them from generating sufficient cashflow to offset stock market acquisition premiums. (It would appear that Imperial Group committed all three errors in its takeover of Howard Johnson.)

1. *Acquirers overestimate the potential for synergy.* Imperial's know-how in consumer goods markets was of little assistance in understanding the US hotel and fast-food markets and HOJO proved to be cash-negative under its new ownership.
2. *Market potential can be overestimated.* Imperial failed to foresee how much of HOJO's hotel business would be lost in the wake of the 1979 oil crisis. At the time of purchase HOJO's rather old-fashioned formula and facilities were already suffering at the hands of the

fast-food chains and speciality restaurants. Located on the major interstate highways, their restaurant and lodging houses were being bypassed by the new breed of travellers and holidaymakers who preferred to fly rather than drive.

Similarly, when General Dynamics paid $670 million for Cessna Aircraft in 1985, it had every reason to believe that the general aviation market would rapidly recover from a cyclical slump in business. It failed to recognise, however, that the overcapacity in the industry was due primarily to structural rather than cyclical factors.

In many instances, the effects of a sudden and unexpected downturn in market demand are so devastating that they outweigh any improvements in performances achieved through post-acquisition rationalisation.

3. *Integration after the takeover is badly handled.* HOJO was unable to attract the more lucrative business traveller because of its family orientation and, under Imperial, failed to move aggressively to reposition its business. Schlumberger also failed dismally in its attempt to compete in the US semiconductor business following its acquisition of Fairchild Semiconductors, Inc.

In all cases a thorough market and competitive analysis in the pre-acquisition period would have revealed many of the problems. Imperial would appear to have made the common mistake of concentrating too heavily on the legal and financial aspects of the acquisition and, as a consequence, underestimated the speed at which US consumer tastes, regional preferences and buying habits can change.

One of McKinsey's contributions to the continuing debate about the pros and cons of 'related' versus 'unrelated' acquisitions is to define a new concept of relatedness which explains the success of Hanson, BTR and other companies in negotiating and digesting takeovers which traditional definitions would classify as unrelated.

In addition to the standard categories of relatedness of industry, technology and markets, McKinsey considers *relatedness of managerial task* to be a key success factor in most takeovers. Thus, Hanson tends to confine its attention to companies with a specific set of attributes even if they happen to be in different industries so that the post-acquisition process is always similar. How is the concept applied in practice?

Hanson's strategy is to buy undervalued companies in basic industries such as food or building materials or predictable, low-tech industries which are unlikely to need new capital. They avoid highly competitive bidding situations, refuse to pay for goodwill and look for assets which can be sold off quickly to recoup the initial investment. They obtain good deals by buying into cyclical businesses that will have good returns over time but happen to be currently out of favour; companies in which one or two divisions have depressed overall performance or companies on the verge of a turnaround but still undervalued by the stock market. Post-acquisition, Hanson moves quickly to decentralise management, pushing responsibility down to the operating level and, usually, dismembering corporate headquarters. They develop incentive schemes which rely on substantial bonuses based on improving profits and return on capital to motivate managers to toe the corporate line. The formula has been successful time and time again.

The human factor in acquisitions

It is evident that many failed acquisitions are due to the neglect of the human consequences of such actions. Those companies that do give priority consideration to the human dimension generally achieve a greater degree of success.

A major 1987 study[7] examined the record of 40 acquisitions by British companies in the UK and the US between 1981 and 1985. Interviews were conducted with over 100 senior executives of the companies concerned. Forty-five per cent of the acquisitions were entirely amicable. A further 45 per cent were partly contested and the remaining 10 per cent were hostile, in that the bid was made over the heads of the vendor company's directors. The study focused on the 'human factor' in takeovers; the way in which both sides handled such issues as who should manage the acquired company, to what extent the two organisations were integrated, and how the new vision and strategy were formulated and communicated.

The interviews with managers from both acquiring and acquired companies revealed a remarkable consensus of opinion on whether a particular takeover was judged to have been successful or not. Fifty-five per cent of the acquisitions were judged by the participants to have been 'very successful' or 'successful', with the remaining 45 per cent regarded as 'so-so', 'unsuccessful' or 'very unsuccessful'.

Which of the human factors made the most difference? The study found that the nature and behaviour of the acquiring company *before* the deal was not of great significance. Neither was the acquiring company's previous experience of takeovers or the relative size of the buyer and seller. Furthermore, although amicable takeovers were generally more successful than hostile takeovers, the difference was not significant.

Surprisingly, it did not make much difference whether or not the purchaser had an advance plan on how to deal with the acquired company. Given that 55 per cent of the acquisitions were judged to be successful, *only one buyer in five had, at the time of purchase, an operational plan of what changes would be needed in the acquired company.*

Of the *pre*-takeover factors only two were found to be significant:

1. the *health* of the company acquired, and
2. whether the acquiring company had carried out a *thorough audit* of its purchase before the takeover.

All the buyers in the study conducted financial audits of the acquired companies prior to purchase but only 37 per cent carried out a *management* or *personnel audit*. These were often quite perfunctory, being confined to pensions, salary levels, personnel policies, etc. Although most buyers emphasised the importance of the purchased company's middle management, 70 per cent did not (or were not able to) meet these managers before the takeover was announced.

The study found that the *post*-acquisition behaviour of the buyer had a critical influence on the success of the acquisition, particularly in dealing with the feelings of *insecurity* which follow all takeovers. In two-thirds of the successful acquisitions, a senior executive from the buying company personally communicated with all levels of the organisation at in-plant meetings, regional conferences or social occasions. In two-thirds of the unsuccessful acquisitions, the buyer did *not* do this.

Two other important factors were the adherence to the assurances given during the takeover negotiations and the provision of investment funds. Both factors created a higher level of commitment and loyalty, especially at middle management level.

Whether or not the acquired company or its departments were merged with those of the purchaser appeared to be of little significance. What was important, however, was the *way* in which such plans were implemented. Success was the result of communicating all decisions clearly and designating individual responsibilities on each side.

Finally, and not without surprise, in two-thirds of *successful* acquisitions, the acquired management reported either performance incentives, better pension entitlements, improved career prospects or the introduction of share options. In two-thirds of *unsuccessful* deals there was a perceived loss or reduction of benefit in one or more of the above areas.

Many of the findings of this study are reflected in the two case studies in an earlier sector of this book.

The search for added value

The acid test for any proposed acquisition is whether or not the purchaser can 'add value' to the acquired company. Far too many acquisitions are *opportunistic* rather than *systematic* and are often the result of an analysis that concentrates on the financial and legal aspects of the transaction at the expense of the all-important strategic issues. It is essential to have a clear understanding of how a particular acquisition will enhance the corporation's overall strategy.

Added value can be created in a number of ways:

1. through *asset synergy:* the ability to achieve economies of scale in production or distribution,
2. through *skills transfer:* the cross-fertilisation of R & D and marketing expertise to create competitive advantage,
3. through the exercise of *market control:* the leverage resulting from improved market share enabling higher unit sales margins, wider distribution and merchandising economies,
4. through *restructuring:* the elimination of duplicate layers of management and the sale of surplus assets to release cash.

It is important to quantify the value creation potential in all of the above areas before completing the acquisition. The mental discipline is demanding but the exercise is fundamental to the negotiations. The calculations should *never* be used as a rationale to raise the purchase price, however. Why should the purchaser pay in advance for the planned synergy when it is the purchaser who will be largely responsible for making it happen?

How does 'added value' work in practice? One simple example will suffice to illustrate the point. It was reported earlier that Imperial had signally failed to add value to their purchase of Howard Johnson. In 1986, Imperial sold Howard Johnson to The Marriott Corporation. Marriott held on to the company-owned restaurants and sold on the company-owned motor lodges as well as the franchised restaurants to Prime Motor Inns. Each of the current owners has been able to add value and create significant synergies. Marriott has improved its market share in the restaurant business and achieved economies of scale in terms of procurement, food distribution and advertising. Prime has created significant management value through its first-hand knowledge of the franchise business plus the provision of already available 'on-site' management for the motor lodges. This, in addition to the fact that the investment base for both parties is now substantially lower, has maximised the chances of successful turnaround.

There is no substitute for experience when it comes to assessing added value. As a general rule, companies which are *less* experienced at acquisitions tend to *overestimate* the synergies arising from them!

Guidelines for success in cross-border acquisitions

Although the final section relates primarily to foreign acquisitions, most of the principles apply equally well to domestic takeovers and, at the same time, summarise many of the main lessons outlined in this book as a whole. To be successful in cross-border acquisitions companies must:

1. *Define their corporate objectives precisely* and articulate an acquisition strategy so that they have a clear idea of what they are looking for.
2. *Analyse and understand how a particular candidate will further these objectives.* An acquisition will only make sense if it creates competitive advantage. It should open up new markets, create economies of scale, bring new technology, create an opportunity to lower production costs or generate economies in distribution.
3. *Analyse the overseas market carefully.* European acquirers should be especially careful not to apply European assumptions to the US environment, remembering that the USA is a large and heterogeneous country where strong regional preferences can create powerful local competitors. Initiate a thorough market and competitive analysis. Major cultural differences also exist between European countries and even within certain nations, e.g. between the French and Flemish-speaking regions of Belgium.
4. *Never overpay in the rush to make an acquisition.* Beware the orchestrated auction and remember that the most attractive prospects should reflect the purchaser's ability to add value to the acquisition. Always be prepared to walk away from a deal.
5. *Never pay for synergy* – it hardly ever happens.
6. *Be prepared to pay a premium for market share.* If acquisition funds are limited, buy 51 per cent of a company with a 30 per cent market share rather than 100 per cent of the equity in a business with only a 10 per cent market share. It is also easier (and much less costly) to manage 'a good, big one' than to sort out the problems of 'a bad, little one'.
7. *Retain local management wherever possible.* Pay particular attention to local compensation and incentive policies and to the subtle cultural differences which can make local management difficult to motivate and control.
8. *Do not attempt to manage an overseas business from your domestic headquarters.* You should have one or more of your own people on the spot on a full-time basis. Distance and culture create obstacles to communication and extra effort is required to build loyalty and mutual trust with local management.
9. *Attempt turnarounds only in industries which you know well.* The combination of a new business activity in an unfamiliar country could be fatal.
10. *Have sufficient management talent on both sides to manage the*

integration process. Thin management cover invariably results in poor execution.

11. *Assign a senior executive to manage the project* and ensure that he has both the authority and resources to do the job.

12. *Prepare a detailed plan for each functional area that needs to be integrated.* The plan should include both reporting relationships and control mechanisms.

Some twenty years ago John Kitching hypothesised a fundamental law for successful acquisitions: 'The sum of management skills must be greater than the joint management task.' This concept has withstood the test of time! Of all the subject-matters considered in the preceding chapters the quality of management is the most critical factor. Only 'managers of change' can release the elusive synergy that is the touchstone of this business. The lesson is quite clear – if you do not have surplus management talent, avoid turnarounds at all costs and be prepared to pay a premium price for companies whose management track record is higher than the industry average.

Happy Hunting!

References

1. Kitching, J. (1967) 'Why do mergers miscarry'. *Harvard Business Review*, November/December. (1974) 'Winning and losing with European acquisitions'. *Harvard Business Review*, March/April.

2. Porter, M. (1987) 'From competitive advantage to corporate strategy'. *Harvard Business Review*, May/June.

3. Peters, Thomas J. and Robert H. Waterman, Jnr (1982) *In Search of Excellence*, New York, (Harper and Row).

4. Rumelt, Richard P. (1974) *Strategy, Structure and Economic Performance.* Boston: Division of Research, Harvard Business School, 1974. Republished as a Harvard Business School Classic; Boston: Harvard Business School Press, 1986.

5. Johanson, J. and Vahlne, J. E. (1977) 'The international process of the firm – a model of knowledge development and increasing foreign market commitments'. *Journal of International Business Studies*, Vol. 8, No. 1.

6. McKinsey & Company (1988) *Shareholder Value Creation in Major Acquisition Programmes*, March.

7. *Acquisitions – the Human Factor* (1987) (London Business School/Egon Zehnder International, March).

Appendix A
Sources of information

General background information

McCarthy's Data Sheets. Available from McCarthy's Information Ltd or in general libraries. Gives full press articles from major newspapers and journals.

Textline Abstracts. Contains articles from international newspapers and journals and is available from Finsbury Data Services.

Financial information

Annual Accounts. Filed at Companies House. It should be noted that filing is often delayed and it may well be 12 months from the last year-end before accounts are available for scrutiny.

Modified accounts for smaller companies are often of little use.

Extel Cards. Available from the London Business School and other major libraries.

Financial Press. Often contains information, opinions and data that vary and may or may not corroborate data already collected. Cuttings are available from the *Financial Times* cutting service, Textline, McCarthy's, etc.

Business Ratios Reports. Available from ICC group and give comparisons with all main participants/competitors in the relevant industry sector.

Brokers' Circulars. Particularly from the target's own stockbroker may conveniently be obtained from a merchant bank with some degree of security.

Market information

Trade Magazines. Contain a great deal of information from unlikely subject headings. Depot or works closures or openings, redundancies, trade press releases and advertisements are added to the data bank.

Trade Associations. Often produce reports on their industry.
May have a library containing useful background information.

Market Research. General reports may be available from organisations
such as Keynote Publications Ltd (ICC Group), Euromonite Publications and Mintel Market Intelligence; business and other major libraries
may also be of help.
In specialist markets, unique research may have to be commissioned.

DTI. UK market and import statistics may be available from SMIL
(Statistics and Market Intelligence Library).

Advertising Spend Data. May be extremely relevant and is available in
quarterly publications from Media Expenditure Analysis Ltd; but such
data are generally only released to advertising practitioners and care
will need to be exercised in securing the data.

Trade Fairs and Exhibitions. Catalogues are a useful source of 'who's
who?' and industry contacts.
'Face-to-face' conversations are best held after hours.

Current trading

Information on current performance and the competition position may
be obtained:
1. directly,
2. through conversation with customers,
3. through conversation with competitors.

Physical assets

Inspection of properties is of key importance, but usually has to be
external. One problem area is that tenure arrangements for individual
properties may be impossible to establish; the accounts will only give an
overall split between freeholds and long and short leaseholds. Information
on throughput, capacity, staffing and general efficiency can often be
gleaned from a simple but, on occasion, prolonged visual inspection.

Appendix B
Due diligence requirements

Contents

I   The core team

II Corporate matters (legal finance tax insurance)
II.1   Corporate
II.2   Intangibles
II.3   Administrative services and related parties
II.4   Regulatory matters
II.5   Legal and miscellaneous matters
II.6   Insurance
II.7   Financial and related matters
II.8   Taxation
II.9   Supplier and expenditure matters
II.10   Facilities and equipment

III Business (US and International)
III.1   Commercial and financial
III.2   Research and development
III.3   Production

IV Environmental matters
IV.1   Environmental and related matters

Annex to Part IV (general due diligence requirements)

V   Employees, employment benefits and labour relations

VI Schedule of site visits

I The core team

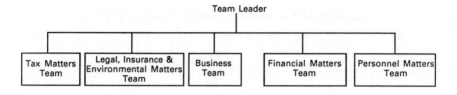

Team Leader

| Tax Matters Team | Legal, Insurance & Environmental Matters Team | Business Team | Financial Matters Team | Personnel Matters Team |

II Corporate matters
(Legal finance tax insurance)

II.1 *Corporate*

Persons responsible
Legal team

Organisational chart, indicating ownership of all companies and branches.

Articles of all companies.

By-laws of all companies.

Minutes of stockholders, boards, committees of all companies.

Jurisdictions and dates of incorporation and qualification of all companies.

Minority interests if any (full details).

Equity investments other than in subsidiaries (descriptive list).

Joint ventures and partnerships (descriptive list, pre-emption rights and copies of material agreements).

Stock-record books of all companies (details of any stock options).

Details of incorporation of any former divisions and of any acquisitions and divestures, including material documentation.

SEC filings, including 10-Ks, 10-Qs, 8-Ks, registration statements and prospectuses, annual reports, annual and special meeting proxy and information statements and Schedule 13Ds.

Details of past securities offerings and bases for exemption.

II.2 Intangibles

Persons responsible
Legal team

Patents – descriptive list of all granted patents, applications and assignments, oppositions including details of registration and copies thereof.

Material improvements to patented know-how (descriptive list).

Trademarks – descriptive list of trademarks, current uses, applications for registration and assignments, including details of registration and copies thereof.

Copyrights – descriptive list of copyrights, applications therefor and assignments, including details of registration.

Licence, royalty and profit-sharing agreements (descriptive list and copies).

Technology-sharing, use and disclosure agreements.

Confidentiality and non-disclosure (policies and forms of agreement).

Material non-patented know-how (descriptive list).

Agreements with employees and others with respect to discoveries and inventions.

Interference, infringement and unfair competition – alleged, latent and actual (descriptive list and material documentation).

Technology subject to US export control or foreign transfer restrictions (descriptive list and summary of restrictions).

Proprietary data – descriptive list of process and other proprietary data, including manuals, formulae, specifications, summaries of test and engineering data, description of use and disclosure limitations.

Customer, employee, supplier and joint venture agreements with respect to proprietary and protected data, improvements, incorporation, disclosure and use.

II.3 Administrative services and related parties

Persons responsible
Legal team

Services provided by non-group affiliates, such as accounting, treasury, data processing, technical, legal and other administrative functions (description on services performed and costs charged).

Service agreements – third party and inter-company – descriptive list including material terms and copies of material agreements.

Transactions with affiliates (descriptive list).

II.4 Regulatory matters

Persons responsible
Legal team

Licences and permits (descriptive schedule identifying licence or permit, relevant authority, term, compliance status and plans).

Security clearances – DOD and technology export control (descriptive list of restrictions and covered information).

EPA, OSHA, CPSC and state and other safety (including private safety testing) regulations (descriptive list of compliance issues, disputes and plans).

FCC, PUC, FERC, FPC, MarAd, OCC, FRB, FDIC, Insurance, Advisers' Act, ABC and DPA registrations and reports.

Government contracts and sub-contracts.

II.5 Legal and miscellaneous matters

Persons responsible
Legal team

Litigation – descriptive list of orders and injunctions in force, as well as pending, threatened and forseeable litigation, proceedings and investigations indicating subject matter, relief sought, status and management assessment, and copies of audit response letters and material correspondence and documents.

Boycott and foreign corrupt practices – copies of compliance policies and description of any issues.

Acquisitions and divestitures – copies of relevant documents, including indemnity agreements.

Contract forms and material agreements – agency/distribution, sales, service, warranty, purchase, non-disclosure and non-use, confidentiality, non-compete, etc.

Purchase contracts, including government contracts (descriptive list) including information concerning acceptance, specification and quality compliance, pricing and audit status; accounting methodology for long-term contracts.

Supply and service commitments and agreements (descriptive list and forms of agreement).

Warranty and quality data – warranty, product testing and quality control policies; quality control logs; warranty experience and dispute data; methodology for accounting purposes.

Foreign operations – description of material restrictions on operations, personnel policies, repatriation of funds, technology, etc.

Consents and other actions necessary in connection with acquisition or change in control – governmental (including foreign) and private.

Descriptive list of assets and operations subject to restrictions on non-US ownership, such as mineral lands leasing, naval petroleum and strategic reserves, state energy and banking, maritime, communications, etc.

Hart–Scott–Rodino notification and report data.

State takeover statutes and regulations.

Descriptive list of operations and assets subject to foreign investment or anti-trust review (e.g. FIRA, AFTRA, Kartellamt, UK-OFT, etc.).

Descriptive list of matters requiring consent for or in connection with an acquisition or change in control.

II.6 *Insurance*

Persons responsible
Legal team

Insurance – descriptive schedule showing risks and amounts covered, policy term, premium rates and periods, carriers, loss experience and coverage disputes, including details of any self-insurance arrangements, future availability of coverage and copies of material policies, in particular:

Full details of:

1. Any major product losses (in excess of $100,000) whether insured or not.
2. Any outstanding litigation relating to the areas of Third Party and Products liability.

3. And in particular:
    (a) any environmental problems and/or litigation; any waste disposal
         sites and/or directives issued by the EPA authorities for the
         clean-up of waste disposal and other sites;
    (b) any Occupational Safety & Health Authority (OSHA) litigation.

Existing insurance programme:

1. How are the insurances handled? Is there a risk/insurance manager
    and to whom does he report? Is there an overall system of safety
    environment?
2. Does Jones have a self-insurance programme, e.g. captive or self-
    insurance schemes for Workers' Compensation, products, etc. or
    alternatively, does Jones carry very high levels of deductibles?
3. Is there an insurance broker, and what are the principal insurance
    company connections?
4. General balance sheet information such as turnover, payroll, etc.

Insurance summary showing:

1. Insurance company.
2. Type of cover.
3. Premiums, renewal dates, details of any long term agreements.
4. Values insured/limits of liability, with a note on the:
    (a) basis of valuation of assets for insurance purposes
    (b) basis of loss settlement procedures.
5. The five-year claims experience for Property Damage, Business
    Interruption and Liability Insurances; particularly in respect of
    pollution.
6. Details of any major losses whether insured or not, covering as wide
    a period as possible.
7. Copies of the major policy wording, i.e. Property Damage, Business
    Interruption and Third Party/Products Liability.
8. Details of Excess Liability protection; limits of cover, markets
    used, etc.

Miscellaneous information:

1. Details of the major products and markets, with particular reference
    to products designed for the aviation, aerospace and nuclear
    industries.
2. Geographic locations of manufacturing operations and an indication
    of any critical suppliers/customers.

II.7 Financial and related matters

Acquisition due diligence objectives

Having determined a purchase price for a business which is based on indicative earnings and cashflow or on net assets, the purchaser must endeavour to confirm that:

1. the after-tax earnings and cashflow assumptions for the business used in the determination are reasonable in relation to its actual past performance and its expected future prospects; and

2. the assets and liabilities (including any liabilities that are not immediately obvious) to be acquired are as assumed and make up all of the assets which historically have provided the profits made by the business. That the assets are in a condition that allows them to meet the assumptions. That actual assets and liabilities are as assumed and that assumptions are based on realistic operating levels taking into account the need to provide for the seasonal nature of the business. That the sellers have not manipulated these in any way and that the business has been operated and managed in a normal manner up to the date of sale (i.e. no artificial promotions and special sales or advertising, maintenance and other cost cutbacks). Profits or cashflows will be available as assumed and no cash will need to be diverted to meet undisclosed or unforeseen costs or liabilities, to increase asset levels in order to operate the business at the assumed rate, or to pay off liabilities that cannot be sustained at the assumed levels (even if provided for in the balance sheet this will require cash outflow).

The people and systems to properly manage the business after the takeover are in place and where necessary arrangements made to keep the essential personnel.

Persons responsible
Financial team

Financial statements – consolidated and consolidating – five years and most recent interim periods (and comparative statements for prior year) together with details of preparation, accounting policies (and changes), intercompany eliminations and transactions with other group members or of a non-recurring nature (e.g. acquisitions and dispositions); copies of normalised, stand-alone statements (including details of head office item allocation and of items not allocated); copies of any statutory financial statements.

Budgets, including capital expenditure, five years and comparative current and prior year interim periods.

Strategic and business plans.

Projections, including assumptions and description of methodology for current year and later periods covered.

Examine:

1. consistency of earnings, costs and profit margins; and
2. fixed and working capital levels over the last five years and obtain understanding of changes and trends.

Compare the indicated future performance with past history; particularly as regards sales levels, profitability, capital expenditure, levels of stocks, debtors, creditors and provisions, tax charges, interest and depreciation charges. Particular attention should be given to items which can be manipulated such as sales, advertising costs, maintenance, overhead allocations, pension contributions and non-recurring items.

Confirm that trading for the period up to the date of sale has been carried on in a normal manner.

Examine provisions, reserves, accrued liabilities, etc., for charges that could relate to the income statement. If levels for credits and provisions cannot be sustained, this could require further investment.

Look at transfer pricing and inter-group charges – confirm that assets and liabilities being acquired are those which historically have provided the income and cashflow of the business.

Look out for lease-backs, other off balance sheet financing, changes to asset valuations and accounting policies.

If business is seasonal, relate assets at acquisition date to average levels when determining value; also take seasonal effect on profits into account in determining profit for the remainder of the initial period.

The following items might also be relevant:

Inventory valuation and accounting methods; recap of last physical inventory by division/location; details of inventory on consignment or off-site; five year and recent interim data, sale or return business.

Backlog data – by product and customer.

Product line data – including allocable asset, revenue, expense and income data.

Assets – listing showing asset types and classes, depreciation methods, lives, cost, accumulated depreciation, basis, potential recapture and location; material re-equipment and replacement plans.

Control, internal audit and management information systems – description, details of any material deficiencies and copies of material documentation.

Management letters, internal accounting control memoranda and control systems reviews from auditors and internal audit staff – five years.

Consultants' and consulting firm studies and reports.

Commodities and foreign exchange procedures and exposures.

Indebtedness, leases and guarantees (descriptive schedule showing type, amount, maturity, rate, principal terms, location of IRB and pollution control facilities; copies of relevant indentures and instruments).

Receivables – descriptive schedule showing customer, amount and aging data; details of bad debt provision and reserve methodology and experience.

Prepaid, accrued and other expenses (description and details) five years and recent interim data.

Bank accounts – listing showing type, purpose, balances and signature authority.

Accountants' and auditors' work papers – financial and tax (all jurisdictions).

Accounting policies and procedures manuals, including consolidation instructions and procedures.

II.8 Taxation

Persons responsible
Tax team

Returns – relevant Federal, state, local and foreign income and revenue tax returns and assessments for periods for which statutory period is open; summary of relevant franchise, payroll and property taxation.

Disputes and open issues (descriptive list and copies of material correspondence and filings and litigation).

Details of penalties levied for delinquent acts.

Status of pending audits and open periods.

Tax planning – description of material tax planning for US and international operations.

Tax holidays.

Tax sharing and indemnity arrangements.

Waivers of limitations periods.

Elections of effect.

Tax accounting for acquisitions.

Asset tax basis data.

Foreign tax credit status, repatriation policy and capitalisation of foreign subsidiaries.

Recapture and step-up data, including appraisals depreciation, ITC, ETC, IDC and foreign E & P.

Earnings and profits data for US and foreign units.

Safe-harbour leasing transactions (descriptive list).

Analysis of deferred income tax account and description of deferred income items.

Financial accounting working papers relating to taxation.

II.9 Supplier and expenditure matters

Persons responsible
Legal team

Principal suppliers – descriptive list showing supplier, products, purchases, terms, alternate sources and adequacy of supply arrangements, including supply of heat, gas and electricity; copies of purchase order forms and material agreements, and material open purchase commitments.

Capital expenditure plans, budgets and engineering studies.

II.10 Facilities and equipment

Persons responsible
Legal team

Facilities – descriptive schedule showing location, use, size, fee or leasehold interest, material restrictions on use.

Leases – real and personal property – descriptive schedule showing property leased, lessor and principal terms, including term, rate, options, cancellation, residual rights and other material provisions and any sub-leases.

Compliance status of facilities, equipment and operations under environmental, safety, zoning and other regulations in effect or proposed.

Title matters – description of material title insurance liens and disputes.

III Business (US and International)

III.1 Commercial and financial

Commercial (including export)

Persons responsible
Business team

1. Review business and strategic plans for:
   (a) marketing plans and reports
   (b) key assumptions on economic and competitive environment
   (c) forecasts for own and competitive products
   (d) reasonableness and thoughtfulness of strategies
   (e) market and competition studies, data and analyses
   (f) US distribution arrangements, contracts, and pricing policies.
2. Determine product sales by product, by market share and by customer to the extent possible.
3. Determine sales/marketing organisation and budget including:
   (a) complement by territory
   (b) advertising and promotional expenditures by-product.
4. Determine complement numbers for overhead functions and assess adequacy of key overhead functions.
5. Determine export sales by product by territory and nature of local organisation.
6. Determine level of commission where sold overseas through local agent.
7. Terms of overseas agency/distribution agreements.

Financial

Persons responsible
Financial team

1. Determine cost structure in sufficient detail to prepare meaningful P & L:
   (a) gross margin by product
   (b) plant fixed costs detail
   (c) detail of overheads level, divisional and corporate expense.
2. Review trading accounts and balance sheet in recent history to determine reason for any abnormalities and suitability as basis for projections.
3. Determine level of debtors and creditors and recent experience.
4. Determine adequacy of accounting systems for control and compatibility with own systems.

III.2 Research and development

Persons responsible
Business team

Research and development

1. Assess commercial/strategic value of intellectual property:
    (a) patents
    (b) development products
    (c) programs, especially those which complement own products.
2. Assess professional competence and innovativeness of organisation.
3. Determine cost structure, budget and complement numbers.
4. Assess rationalisation opportunities in combination with self and potential mobility of people.
5. Assess condition of physical plant; estimate real estate value of properties.

Registration

Determine status of registration of current products and assess registration program/timetable of development portfolio.

Licensing agreement

Determine ownership of technology and licence arrangements for exploiting or supporting it.

Toxicological and environmental issues

1. Determine extent and impact of toxicological and environmental issues.
2. Assess toxicological testing capability.

III.3 Production

Persons responsible
Business team

Technology and engineering

1. Assess competitiveness of technology.
2. Assess status of existing plant facilities:
    (a) capacity and occupacity
    (b) adequacy of support facilities.

3. Source of key raw materials and intermediates.
4. Assess difficulty in separating agchem assets from other facilities, physically, and supplies and services.
5. Determine capital budget:
   (a) maintenance and replacement
   (b) major expansions/savings projects
   (c) normal level of sustenance expenditures.

Environmental

Assess adequacy of health, safety and environmental systems and controls (including potential liabilities from past practices).

Cost accounting

1. Provide breakdown of plant costs.
2. Provide breakdown of stocks level by product and by raw material, work-in-progress and finish product.
3. Assess adequacy of cost accounting systems.

Personnel and labour relations

1. Manpower numbers and split.
2. View of labour relations/unions.

IV Environmental matters

IV.1 Environmental and related matters

Persons responsible
Environmental team

Emission, discharge, disposal, generation, transportation and handling of toxic and hazardous substances and pollutants – descriptive list of substances and volumes, methods and sites

Substance and other licences, permits and standards – descriptive list and copies, including information concerning proposed standards, plans, compliance programs and relevant dates

Disposal contractors – descriptive list of contractors, substances disposed and disposal standards

Environmental incidents – copies of policies, historical reports, analyses, enforcement actions and settlements

Compliance issues, disputes and litigation – actual, threatened, past or foreseeable – descriptive list and copies of analyses, studies and material correspondence, notices, reports, litigation papers and status of settlement discussions

Compliance programs – descriptive list and material engineering and cost data

Superfund sites – descriptive list of sites for which the group (or others for which the group may have responsibility) have received notices or orders for which group may be responsible

Health and environmental studies of relevant substances and processes and effects thereof

Descriptive list of environmental liability and loss insurance and indemnities including copies thereof

Environmental audit – Has Jones had performed, internally or externally, any environmental audits of any or all of its operations or facilities – US or abroad? If so, please provide the relevant information.

Waste disposal matters – these questions attempt to elicit information on Jones's waste disposal activities and involvement at waste facilities.

1. Identify the number of Superfund sites with which Jones is 'associated' and describe the basis on which Jones is considered to be 'associated' with these sites.
2. What is the status of these sites? Have Remedial Investigations/Feasibility Studies been made or Records of Decision issued on the sites?
3. What is Jones's known, asserted or estimated percentage involvement or allocation for each of the sites? Who else is involved?
4. Apart from these sites, what other sites is Jones aware of where federal, state or private parties have requested information as indications of possible involvement by Jones?
5. Are there any private third-party actions involving Jones associated with any of Jones's waste treatment, storage or disposal sites? If so, what are the details, e.g. number of plaintiffs, claims, relief sought, etc.?
6. What is the status of the insurance coverage for these and other sites? Does Jones have any EIL coverage? Under all insurance what are the limits of liability and retention? Who are the carriers?

Hazardous waste – these questions primarily look at the current operations for compliance with the Resources Conservation and Recovery Act (RCRA).

1. Do all hazardous waste treatment, storage and disposal facilities have interim status under RCRA? If not, why? Have all part B applications been filed as requested? If not, why? What is the status of these applications?
2. Do any existing operations presently have or anticipate enforcement actions imposed upon them by EPA or state authorities?
3. Have any operations been inspected by EPA or state agencies regarding compliance with applicable regulations? If so, what was the result – fines, penalties, administrative or consent orders, etc.? Have there been any citizen suits brought? If so, describe.
4. Have any facilities received request from EPA for information as to on-site releases of hazardous substances or waste disposal under the provisions of Section 3007 of RCRA?

Water – the following address compliance issues under the Clean Water Act and related statutes.

1. Do all operations have currently valid water discharge permits? Are the operations in compliance with such permits? If not, what are the problems?
2. Have any operations been inspected by EPA or state agencies regarding compliance with applicable regulations? If so, what was the result – fines, penalties, administrative or consent orders, etc.? Have there been any citizen suits brought? If so, describe.
3. Do any of the operations have injection or deep wells? If so, have the requisite permits been obtained, e.g. underground injection control and what is the status of such permits? Are any such facilities subject to significant modification or termination requirements?

Air – the following seek information on compliance and growth potential under the Clean Air Act and related statutes.

1. Do all operations have currently valid air discharge permits? Are the operations in compliance with such permits? If not, what are the problems?
2. Have any operations been inspected by EPA or state agencies regarding compliance with applicable regulations? Are there any enforcement actions anticipated or pending or any fines, penalties, administrative or consent orders, etc. arising out of these matters? Have there been any citizen suits brought? If so, describe.
3. Are any operations in a non-attainment area?
4. Are any operations faced with the need to make significant alterations of plant facilities or provisions to meet more stringent air emission regulations or operating under interim variance provisions?

Occupational safety and health – these questions ask how Jones is doing on compliance with in-plant health and safety requirements under the Occupational Safety and Health Act or the Mine Safety and Health Act.

1. What is the compliance status of all operations regarding worker health and safety? What is the history of OSHA/MSHA inspections? How many citations have been issued in the past for wilful, repeat or criminal violations? If any, describe. Are there are outstanding citations?

2. What is the status of compliance regarding the Hazard Communication Standard? Do all covered facilities have in place a written hazard communication program? Have all labels and Material Safety Data Sheets been prepared thereunder? Have any of the operations received OSHA citations for non-compliance? If so, describe.

Toxic substances – the following examine Jones's compliance under the Toxic Substances Control Act (TSCA).

1. Has Jones or any of its operations had an inspection under the Toxic Substances Control Act? If so, describe.

2. Has Jones manufactured or imported any chemical substance within the past five years which is or has been the subject of investigation or enforcement by EPA regarding pre-manufacturing requirements under Section 5 of TSCA?

3. Has Jones submitted any Section 8(e) notices under TSCA? If so, describe. What was done as a result?

4. Is Jones presently subject to any consent order or similar agreement between it and EPA relating to the manufacture and/or use of any chemical substance under TSCA?

Tort litigation

1. Is Jones involved in any 'toxic tort' litigation? What is the history and status of its product liability litigation? Please describe. Is Jones involved in any class action litigation? If so, describe.

2. What current outstanding litigation or administrative actions are there against Jones? Describe.

Annex to Part IV
General due diligence requirements
Commercial

1. *Products*
Product lists, literature, specifications, manuals, pricing, sales and backlog data.

Sales analysis by products and product groups with as much historical data as is achievable.

Direct R & D expenditure in support of Products – itemise and analyse.

Licences affecting the production/marketing of any product.

Patents held on any product or process.

Any distribution agreements – terms, duration and termination provisions.

2. *Customers*
Customer lists showing sales and backlog by product.

Sales contracts including any government contracts – descriptive list, including information concerning duration, termination provisions, acceptance, specification and quality compliance, pricing any audit status; accounting methodology where appropriate on long-term contracts.

Sales contracts/arrangements with other parts of company. Terms as above with particular emphasis on duration, termination provisions and existing pricing arrangements.

Supply and service commitments and agreements – descriptive lists and forms of agreement.

Warranty and quality data – warranty, product testing and quality control policies, quality control logs, warranty experience and dispute data; methodology for accounting purposes.

Any expected changes in customer base.

Geographic analysis of product sales, revenue, expense and income both inside the USA and outside.

Distribution arrangements – dealers, distributors and agents – descriptive list including product and sales data and copies and forms of agreement especially details of commissions and termination dates.

Receivables – schedule showing details of debt by customers with aging data, and information on bad debt provision and reserve methodology and experience.

3. *Market/competitor*
Market and competition studies, data and analysis.

Market share data by-product/market segment.

4. *Supply and logistics*
Principal suppliers – descriptive list showing supplier, products, purchases, terms, alternative sources and adequacy of supply

arrangements, including supply of heat, gas and electricity, copies of purchase order forms and material agreements, material open purchase commitments terms duration and termination provisions.

Specifically supply arrangements with other parts of company and terms duration, pricing provision (and accounting practices) termination provisions.

Transportation arrangements (in and out).

Creditors – analysis of current creditors, historical data.

Stock levels – itemised by products any provisions relating to sub-standard or slow moving stock.

5. *Marketing policy*
    Marketing and price policies and manuals.

    Marketing plans and reports.

    Product and project proposals – plans and engineering studies.

    Advertising and promotional expenditures by product.

6. *Fixed expenses*
    Analysis of production fixed expenses, especially maintenance.

    Analysis of overhead expenditure by functions.

    Analysis of overhead expenditure allocated to the business of company. Accounting basis of allocation.

    Schedule of depreciation charge.

7. *Cash*
    State of repair of current asset base.

    Historical fixed capital expenditure data with particular emphasis on sustenance/maintenance capital.

    Capital expenditure plans, budgets and engineering studies.

Production

1. *Production/engineering data*
    Plant capacity and current output (by major product).

    Plant operating costs (budget and actual).

    Process descriptions.

    Listing of all raw materials.

    Listing of all products produced.

    Tolling arrangements (if any).

Current and three year capital expenditure projections (list of all projects in excess of $100,000).

Utility sources (obtain purchase agreements, contracts, etc.).

Utility demands and capacities.

Waste disposal/treatment facilities and/or methods.

Maintenance/service:
(a) how supplied – in-house/contract
(b) list of o/s service contracts (waste hauliers/traders, etc.).

Plant drawings (plot plans, aerial photos, topo's, etc.).

Description of buildings and structures.

Condition of buildings and structures.

Description of idle facilities.

Zoning and land use restrictions:
(a) any current permit/licence problems (obtain list of permits & permitting authority)
(b) any changes anticipated
(c) industrial district restrictions, etc.

Operating permit requirements if any and status of same (NPDES, local, state, etc.).

Information regarding any hazardous processes or operations.

Listing of any current or anticipated regulatory citations/litigation and status of same.

Listing of taxing authorities and annual assessments.

Emergency response provisions, i.e.:
(a) fire
(b) ambulance
(c) medical.

2. *Health and environmental safety*
Are there any major potential problems/risks and liabilities:
(a) what substances are used/produced/emitted/disposed and:
   (i)   what are the significant health hazards of these
   (ii)   what is or has been employee exposure to same
   (iii) current measurements and controls
(b) impact of (a) on neighbourhood
(c) what is and/or has been waste disposal practice:
   (i)   obtain list of disposal sites
   (ii)   are any on superfund list
   (iii) if on site disposal/treatment done – check adequacy

(d) obtain RCRA notification lists

(e) what PMN, FDA mechanisms exist

(f) what are MSDS/LABEL procedures

Determine systems/procedures in place for:

(a) hygiene/health
   (i)   does a program exist that measures employee exposure
   (ii) does a program exist that provides medical information if required

(b) environmental permitting:
   (i)   obtain list of permits for air, water, RCRA (TSO), etc.
   (ii) obtain list of all waste discharges – characterisation, etc.

(c) who handles local/state, federal matters

(d) what loss prevention programs (fire, explosion, HAZOP) are in place

(e) list any fires, explosions in last five years

(f) obtain OSHA logs, citations, etc.

(g) list any major environmental emission in last three years.

3. *Industrial relations*
Copies of all labour contracts to include wages and benefits.

Copies of all benefit plan booklets. If booklets are not available, copies of plan descriptions.

A listing, including current status, of all Employee Relations charges currently open against the company including EEO, ADEA, ERISA, NLRB, etc.

Copies of handbooks for all non-union sites. If handbooks are not available, wage, benefit and any other employee related policy and procedure written information.

If available, divisional personnel policy and procedure manual.

A listing of Employee Relations management professionals by site, including divisional headquarters.

Organisation charts, employment contracts and any available information relative to whether or not key management personnel would continue with new owner.

4. *General observations*
Walk plant to obtain impression of general conditions.

Observe water (potable/fire) supply and source.

Inspect utility (steam/electricity) generating/distribution facilities.

Observe waste storage, treating handling facilities.

General observation of production facilities and equipment.

Inspect process control laboratory facilities.

Inspect on-site R & D activity.

Determine how/who customer service problems handled.

V Employees, employment benefits and labour relations

Persons responsible
Personnel team

Organisational chart indicating functions and reporting responsibilities.

List of employees showing name, age, starting date, responsibilities, compensation, prior service and intent (if any) to retire or resign.

Schedule of material changes in compensation in last year.

Severance terms.

Employment and consultants' agreements – descriptive list and copies.

Confidentiality policy and forms of agreement.

Union contracts – descriptive list (including re-negotiation, expiration, escalation and other provisions involving prospective changes) and copies.

Union representation, certification and election matters – descriptive list.

Labour disputes, grievances, arbitrations, unfair labour practices and litigation – descriptive list of all material matters.

Equal employment, age and occupational safety and health matters – disputes, complaints, investigations and other proceedings details thereof and proposed compliance programs.

Overhead structure.

Personnel manuals and policies – copies.

Policies – vacations, severance, transfer and other material personnel policies, copies or descriptive list (for unwritten policies).

Pension and similar plans (including multi-employer plans) descriptive list showing participant classes, benefits payable, plan assets, vested and accrued benefits, contributions (historical and projected) and copies of plans, plan descriptions and financial and actuarial reports and assumptions.

Pension funding.

Incentive and similar benefit arrangements (including profit-sharing, thrift option, s.a.r. and performance plans) descriptive list showing participants, benefits payable, contributions (historical and projected) and copies of plans and plan descriptions.

Health, welfare, disability and similar benefit plans and insurance programs (including union plans) same information as for incentive arrangements, including experience and prospective cost data and descriptive list and copies of any underlying insurance policies, including any retrospective rating information.

Workmen's compensation – summary of historical loss and prospective and retrospective rating changes.

Foreign regulation of personnel policies, pensions and benefits.

VI Schedule of site visits

Persons Responsible	Sites	Date of Visit

Appendix C
Extract from the City Code on
Takeovers and Mergers

General principles*

Introduction

It is impracticable to devise rules in sufficient detail to cover all circumstances which can arise in offers. Accordingly, persons engaged in offers should be aware that the spirit as well as the precise wording of the General Principles and the ensuing Rules must be observed. Moreover, the General Principles and the spirit of the Code will apply in areas or circumstances not explicitly covered by any Rule.

While the boards of the offeror and the offeree company and their respective advisers have a duty to act in the best interests of their respective shareholders these General Principles and the ensuing Rules will, inevitably, impinge on the freedom of action of boards and persons involved in offers; they must, therefore, accept that there are limitations in connection with offers on the manner in which the pursuit of those interests can be carried out.

Each director of an offeror and of the offeree company has a responsibility to ensure, so far as he is reasonably able, that the Code is complied with in the conduct of an offer . . . . Financial advisers have a particular responsibility to comply with the Code and to ensure, so far as they are reasonably able, that an offeror and the offeree company, and their respective directors, are aware of their responsibilities under the Code and will comply with them. Financial advisers should ensure that the Panel is consulted whenever relevant and should cooperate fully with any enquiries made by the Panel. Financial advisers must also be mindful of conflicts of interest . . . .

General principles

1.   All shareholders of the same class of an offeree company must be treated similarly by an offeror.

2.   During the course of an offer, or when an offer is in contemplation, neither an offeror, nor the offeree company, nor any of their respective advisers may furnish information to some shareholders which is not made available to all shareholders.

This principle does not apply to the furnishing of information in confidence by the offeree company to a *bona fide* potential offeror or vice versa.

3.   An offeror should only announce an offer after the most careful and responsible consideration. Such an announcement should be made only when the offeror has every reason to believe that it can and will continue to be able to implement the offer: responsibility in this connection also rests on the financial adviser to the offeror.

4.   Shareholders must be given sufficient information and advice to enable them to reach a properly informed decision and must have sufficient time to do so. No relevant information should be withheld from them.

5.   Any document or advertisement addressed to shareholders containing information or advice from an offeror or the board of the offeree company or their respective advisers must, as is the case with a prospectus, be prepared with the highest standards of care and accuracy.

6.   All parties to an offer must use every endeavour to prevent the creation of a false market in the securities of an offeror or the offeree company. Parties involved in offers must take care that statements are not made which may mislead shareholders or the market.

7.   At no time after a *bona fide* offer has been communicated to the board of the offeree company, or after the board of the offeree company has reason to believe that a *bona fide* offer might be imminent, may any action be taken by the board of the offeree company in relation to the affairs of the company, without the approval of the shareholders in general meeting, which could effectively result in any *bona fide* offer being frustrated or in the shareholders being denied an opportunity to decide on its merits.

8.   Rights of control must be exercised in good faith and the oppression of a minority is wholly unacceptable.

9.   Directors of an offeror and the offeree company must always, in advising their shareholders, act only in their capacity as directors and not have regard to their personal or family shareholdings or to their personal relationships with the companies. It is the shareholders' interests taken as a whole, together with those of employees and creditors, which should be considered when the directors are giving advice to shareholders.

10.   Where control of a company is acquired by a person, or persons acting in concert, a general offer to all other shareholders is normally required; a similar obligation may arise if control is consolidated. Where an acquisition is contemplated as a result of which a person may incur such an obligation, he must, before making the acquisition, ensure that he can and will continue to be able to implement such an offer.

Appendix D
Preliminary information on target companies

Note: This list is not comprehensive and should be tailored to particular transactions. It should follow the sequence of the Warranties so that the information made available can form the basis of the Disclosure Letter.

General information

Business summary

A copy of any document that may be available that contains a summary of the business of the company and a diagram of the Group structure.

Particulars of the company

Registered no:
Registered office:
Date and place of incorporation:
Authorised capital:
Issued capital:
Directors:
Secretary:
Accounting reference date:
Auditors:

Shareholders	No. of shares	%	Issue date

Particulars (as above) of any subsidiaries

Particulars of related companies

(Name, registered office, place of incorporation and percentage shareholding only.)

Memorandum and Articles of Association

Copies of the complete Memorandum and Articles of Association of the company and any subsidiaries.

Business assets

Plant, etc.

A schedule of all major items of plant, machinery and equipment and all motor vehicles used, owned or leased by the company and (separately) each subsidiary (distinguish assets owned and those leased – see also below).

Hire purchase and leasing

A schedule of any hire purchase or finance leasing contracts including a note of the amounts outstanding under them of the company and (separately) each subsidiary.

Charges

Details of any liens, mortgages, charges or encumbrances over the assets of the company and (separately) each subsidiary (except those relating to properties and listed on page 174).

Licences and consents

Details of any key licences or consents necessary for the business(es) of the company and (separately) each subsidiary.

Intellectual property

Details of all intellectual property (patents, trade marks, copyrights, know-how, computer software, etc.):

1. owned by the company or a subsidiary
2. used by the company or a subsidiary under licence
3. licensed to third parties by the company or a subsidiary

Litigation

Details of all pending or threatened litigation (minor debt collection may be referred to in the aggregate) against the company or any subsidiary.

Accounts

Audited accounts

Copies of the audited accounts of the company and each subsidiary for the last three years together with copies of the consolidated accounts for the same period.

Management accounts

Copies of the unaudited management accounts of the company and the subsidiaries for the period from the date of the last audited accounts to date.

Accounting policies

Details of any changes in the accounting policies over the last three years.

Capital commitments

Details of all capital commitments incurred by the company or any subsidiary since the last audited accounts.

Commercial

Standard terms

Copies of all standard terms and conditions of business of the company and each subsidiary.

Material contracts

Copies of all material contracts to which the company or any subsidiary is a party.

Intra group contracts

Copies of any agreements between the company and the seller or between it or its subsidiaries and the seller or the seller's subsidiaries.

Agencies, etc.

Details of agency, distribution, franchise or similar arrangements granted

1. by the company or any subsidiary
2. to the company or any subsidiary

Trade associations

Is the company or any subsidiary a member of any trade association?

Competition law

Is the company or any subsidiary party to any agreement or arrangements registered under the Restrictive Trade Practices Act 1976 or notified under Article 85 of the Treaty of Rome or any agreement or arrangement which ought to be so registered or notified?

Financial

Dividends

Have any dividends been declared or paid since the date of the last audited accounts?

Bank borrowings

1. Name and address of bankers.
2. Current borrowing limit(s).
3. Amount outstanding on overdraft (company and each subsidiary).

Other borrowings

Details of all other borrowings of the company and each subsidiary including loan capital, acceptances and debt factoring, and guarantees of borrowings.

Loans

Details of all loans made by the company and each subsidiary.

Guarantees and contingent liabilities

Copies of any guarantees, indemnities or suretyships given by or on behalf of the company or any subsidiary and details of any contingent liabilities outstanding.

Insurance

Insurance

A schedule of current insurances of the company and each subsidiary with particulars of (i) renewal dates, (ii) annual premiums, (iii) amount of cover, (iv) property covered, (v) the nature of the risks, (vi) the name of the relevant insurance company and (vii) the policy number.

Insurance claims

Are any insurance claims outstanding and unsettled?

Taxation

Tax returns

Have all Corporation Tax, VAT, PAYE and other tax returns been made and agreed?

Tax payments

Has all such tax due been punctually paid?

Disputes

Are there any matters in dispute or under discussion with the Inland Revenue or HM Customs & Excise?

Capital gains

Are there any assets in respect of which the 'cost' for Capital Gains Tax purposes is materially different from the actual cost to the company or any subsidiary?

Close companies

Has the company or any subsidiary ever been a 'close company' for tax purposes?

Groups of companies

Has the company always been a member of a group of companies; have there been any intra group transfers of assets?

Group income election

Is there a group income election in force relating to the payment of dividends/interest?

Properties

Good and marketable title

Particulars of title(s) including a plan and copies of all lease(s) abstracts of title and tenure, rents and rent charges, etc. of properties owned, controlled or occupied by the company and each subsidiary.

Free from encumbrances

Details of any encumbrances and third party rights.

Unusual restrictions

Are there any unusual restrictions?

Rents

Have all rents and service charges (if applicable) been paid to the last due date?

User

Details of any planning restrictions which would affect the carrying on at any premises of the business now carried on there by the company or any subsidiary.

Planning consents

Details of any work carried out at any premises since they were acquired by the company or subsidiary which would require planning or other consents.

Notices

Copies of any notices been served by any public authority in respect of any of the premises; have such notices been complied with?

Repair

Copies of valuations and surveys of any of the properties.

Disputes

Details of any disputes relating to the properties.

Employees

Particulars of employees

List all employees' principal particulars of employment:
Name:
Address:
Job title:
Salary:
Age:
Sex:
Notice period:
Period of continuous employment:
Form of contract:

Forms of contract

Copies of any standard form contract(s) for employees.

Senior executives and directors

Copies of contracts of employment of all directors and senior employees
([£   ] per annum or above) and of all employees not on the standard
form contract(s) supplied.

Compensation

Has any compensation been agreed to be paid to any director, ex-director,
employee or ex-employee (or their dependants)?

Bonus schemes

Details of any scheme for commission or remuneration based on turnover,
profits or sales.

Share option schemes

Details of any share option or shadow share option scheme which is not
included under bonus schemes (above).

Labour relations

Details of trade union agreements.

Industrial disputes

Details of any disputes with employees or industrial action past, pending or threatened.

Employees' loans

Details of any loans to or by employees.

Pensions

Scheme

A description of any pension scheme(s) together with copy documentation for the scheme(s).

Actuarial valuation(s) (where applicable)

Copies of the most recent actuarial valuations of any pension schemes.

Approval

Have all schemes been approved by the Inland Revenue?

Index

accounting, 171
  acquisition and merger, 39–42
  pensions, 91
acquisition, xiii–xiv, 1–2
  City Code on Takeovers, 167–8
  due diligence requirements, 145–66
  evaluating for, 47–60
  failure of, xiii–xiv, 2, 132
  financial valuation methods, 29–46
  financing, 42–6, 79
  finding suitable businesses, 16–28
  information sources, 143–4
  legal aspects of, 73–84
  management after, 120–31
  mistakes, 134–6
  negotiation, 61–72
  pensions and incentive schemes, 85–106
  preliminary information on target
      companies, 169–76
  public relations, 107–19
  reasons for, 11–12, 108, 113, 123
  risk minimisation, 132–42
  strategy, 1–15, 47, 151
added value, 50–2, 139–40
Additional Voluntary Contributions
    (AVCs), 88, 106
advisers, 14, 76–7
  finding suitable businesses, 21–4
  PR, 117–18
Agreement, acquisition, 79–80
  pension clause, 92–4
Allday, John, ix, 29–46
Angear, Thomas R., ix, xiii–xiv, 132–42
announcement of takeover, 110–15
  and management, 122–3
assets basis of valuation, 35–7

break-up, 35–6
  investment, 35
  significance of assets, 36–7
Atlantic Sea Products, 49
auction process, 25, 56–7
Australia, 80

BAT Industries, 7
BTR, 2, 11, 50, 135, 137
Belmont, E.M., ix–x, 85–106
bonuses, see incentive schemes
Booker, acquisitions, 48–54
  adding value, 50–2
  cashflow, 52–4
  sources, 49–50
  synergy, strategy, simplicity, 50
break-up basis of valuation, 35–6
brokers, 21–2
Buckingham v. Francis, 38

Canada, 80
capitalisation factor, 32–4
cashflow, 38–9, 52–4
Cessna Aircraft, 137
City Code on Takeovers and Mergers, 78,
    167–8
City, the, 110, 116
'closure' of negotiation, 71–2
Collins, Stephen, 106
commercial matters, company information,
    160–2, 171–2
community, local, 111
Companies Act 1985, 40, 42, 78
competition, 75–6
competitive advantage, 5–6
conglomerate acquisitions, 133

consideration, 43–5, 78–9
consultants, M&A, 22
contested bids, 116–17
Contracted Out Money Purchase Scheme
    (COMP), 88
corporate matters, due diligence
    requirements, 146–54
Council of the Stock Exchange, 78
Country Kitchen Foods, 49
Crocker National Bank, 134
cross-border acquisitions, see international
    acquisitions
cultural differences, 141

Daehnfeldt, 49
Dewhurst, John, x, xiii–xiv, 47–60
Disclosure Letter, 82–3
discounted cashflow
    analysis, 52–4
    approach to valuation, 38–9
distance, geographical and psychological,
    133–4
diversification, 7–8, 10
    controlled, 132–3
    errors, 135
due diligence procedures, ICI, 57–9, 145–66
    business, 155–7
    commercial matters, 160–2
    core team, 146
    corporate matters, 146–54
        facilities etc., 154
        financial, 151–3
        insurance, 149–50
        legal, 148–9
        regulatory, 148
        taxation, 153–4
    employees, 165–6
    environmental matters, 157–60
    production, 162–5

'earn-outs', 79
earnings basis of valuation, 30–4
    capitalisation factor, 32–4
    maintainable profits, 30–2
Elder, Ian F., x, 73–84
employees
    information on, 165–6, 175–6
    PR, 111
    transfer of, 74
    see also management; incentive schemes;
        pensions

environmental matters, 157–60
Euromonite Publications, 144
European Economic Community (EEC)
    common market, xiii
    employment transfer, 74
    merger controls, 76
    Treaty of Rome, 172
evaluation of companies for acquisition,
    47–60
    Booker, 48–54
        adding value, 50–2
        cashflow, 52–4
        sources of acquisitions, 49–50
        synergy, strategy, simplicity, 50
    financial, see financial valuation methods
    ICI, 54–60
        auction process, 56–7
        decision, 59–60
        due diligence procedures, 57–9,
            145–66
        large acquisitions, 55
        strategic review, 56
Eversheds, 49
executive share option schemes, 101

failure of takeovers, xiii–xiv, 2, 132–42
    added value, 139–40
    common mistakes, 134–6
    cross-border, 140–2
    distance, geographical and psychological,
        133–4
    human factor, 138–9
    relatedness, 136–8
Fairchild Semiconductors Inc., 137
final salary type of pension, 86–7
Finance Act 1970, 94
Finance Act 1978, 100
Finance Act 1980, 101
Finance Act 1984, 101
Finance Act 1986, 90
Finance (No.2) Act 1987, 99
financial matters, company information,
    151–3, 172
financial valuation methods, 29–46
    acquisition and merger accounting,
        39–42
    assets basis, 35–7
        break-up, 35–6
        investment, 35
        significance of assets, 36–7
    discounted cashflow, 38–9

financial valuation methods (*continued*)
  earnings basis, 30–4
    capitalisation factor, 32–4
    maintainable profits, 30–2
    financing acquisitions, 42–6
    super-profits approach, 37–8
    trade practices, 39
    see also evaluation
financing acquisitions, 42–6, 79
  cash, 44–5
  leveraged acquisitions, 46
  shares, 44
  taxation, 45
  terms, 43
  timing of payment, 43
'finders', 21
finding suitable businesses, 16–28
  brokers, 21–2
  cross-border, 26–7
  fees, 23–4
  financial advisers, 23
  M&A consultants, 22
  management of search process, 24–6
  sources of ideas, 17–21
    external, 19–21
    internal, 17–19

General Dynamics, 137

Hanson Trust, 2, 50, 135, 137–8
Hart–Scott–Rodino Antitrust
    Improvements Act (USA), 75
Heads of Agreement/Letters of Intent, 76
horizontal acquisitions, 133
hostile takeovers, 77–8
Howard Johnson, 134, 136–7, 140
human factor in takeovers, 138–9
Hursts, 49

ICI, 48, 54–60
  acquisitions, 54–60
    auction process, 56–7
    decision, 59–60
    due diligence procedures (*q.v.*), 57–9,
      145–66
    large acquisitions, 55
    strategic review, 56
Imperial Group, 134, 136–7, 140
incentive schemes, 98–106
  bringing new company into existing
    scheme, 102–3

cash schemes, 98–9
choice of, 101–2
deferred bonuses, 105–6
pension planning, 106
Profit-related Pay (PRP), 99–100
share schemes, 100–2
  executive, 101
  profit-sharing, 100–1
  savings-related, 101–2
  target company with own share scheme,
    103–4
  transfer pricing, 104
  triggers, 105
  unapproved schemes, 105
  warehouse trust, 106
Income and Corporation Taxes Act 1988,
  94
indemnification, 83
information, preliminary, on target
    companies, 6, 169–76
  accounts, 171
  business assets, 170
  commercial, 171–2
  employees, 175–6
  financial, 172
  general, 169–70
  insurance, 172–3
  litigation, 170
  pensions, 176
  properties, 174–5
  requirements, ICI, 145–66
  sources, 143–4
  taxation, 173
Institute of Public Relations, 118
insurance, company information, 149–50,
  172–3
insured pension schemes, 92
intermediaries in acquisition, 20–4, 27–8
  brokers, 21–2
  fees, 23–4
  financial advisers, 23
  M&A consultants, 22
international acquisitions, 26–7, 140–2
investment basis of valuation, 35

Johanson, J., 133–4
junk-bond market, 46

Keynote Publications Ltd, 144
Kitching, John, 120, 132, 142

legal aspects of acquisitions, 73–84
  advisers, 76–7
  Agreement, 79–80
  competition and other regulatory
    approvals, 75–6
  Disclosure Letter, 82–3
  Heads of Agreement/Letters of Intent, 76
  indemnification, 83
  jurisdictions, 75
  legal status of seller, 74
  legal status of target, 73
  management of the company, 83–4
  price, 78–9
  purchase of a business, 74–5
  quoted and unquoted companies, 77–8
  warranties, 80–2
legal matters, company information, 148–9,
  170
legislation
  competition, 75–6, 78, 172
  incentive schemes, 99–101
  merger relief, 40, 42
  pensions, 86–8, 90, 94
'Lehman scale', 24
Letters of Intent/Heads of Agreement, 76
leveraged acquisitions, 46
Leverhulme, Lord, xiii
Linfood, 49
Loseley, 49

McCarthy's Data Sheets, 143
McKinsey & Co., 136–7
McNabs, 49
maintainable profits, 30–2
management, legal aspects of acquisitions,
  83–4
management, post-acquisition, 120–31
  announcement, 122–3
  communications, 125
  plan, 126–31
    business, 126
    financial control, 128–9
    organisational structure, 126–7
    personnel policy and management
      style, 127–8
    production, 130–1
    research and development, 129–30
    sales and marketing, 130
  post-acquisition control, 123–4
  pre-implementation, 121–2
  transitional period, 124–5

Marriott Corporation, 140
Media Expenditure Analysis Ltd, 144
media, PR, 111–12, 114, 115
merger controls, 75–6
Michaels, David, x, 61–72
Midland Bank, 134
Middlebrook, 49
Mintel Market Intelligence, 144
money purchase type of pension, 87–8
Monopolies and Mergers Commission, 75,
  117

Nature's Best, 49
negotiation, 60, 61–72
  completion, 71–2
  inception, 62–3
  and management, 121–2
  meetings, 64
  and PR, 109–10
  price, 66–8
    packaging, 68
    strategy, 67–8
  process, 65–6
  reading and controlling a situation, 64–5
  status of parties, 63–4
  strategies, 68–71
    deadlock, 70–1
    good guy/bad guy, 69–70
    immovable mountain, 70
    referring back, 70
    tough approach, 69

Occupational Pensions Board, 86
Office of Fair Trading, 117

Panel on Takeovers and Mergers, 78
pensions, 85–98
  accounting for, 91
  Additional Voluntary Contributions
    (AVCs), 88, 106
  Contracted Out Money Purchase Scheme
    (COMP), 88
  disclosure, 94–5
  final salary type, 86–7
  Free-Standing AVCs, 88
  funds, 89–90
  insured schemes, 92
  levelling up, 95–6
  liabilities, 85–6, 91–2
  money purchase type, 87
  non-pensionable employees, 96
  Personal Pension (PP) contracts, 88

pensions (*continued*)
  planning, 106
  redundancies, 97
  sale agreement clause, 92–4
  schemes, 85–9
  SERPS, 87–8
  strategy, 95–7
  surpluses, 90
  taxation, 93–4
  trusts, 86
Personal Pension (PP) contracts, 88
Peters, Thomas J., 132
Porter, Professor Michael, 48, 132, 135–6
price, 78–9
  negotiation, 66–71
Prime Motor Inns, 140
production, information, 162–5
Profit-related Pay (PRP), 99–100
profit-sharing share schemes, 100–1
public relations (PR), 107–19
  beginning, 107–8
  and the City, 110, 116
  community, 111
  contested bids, 116–17
  employees, 111
  external advice, 117–18
  media, 111–12, 114, 115
  phases, 108–16
    negotiation, 109–10
    announcement, 110–15
    aftermath, 116
    planning, 112–14
  reasons for takeover, 108, 113, 119
  spokesperson, 107

quoted and unquoted companies, legal
  aspects of acquisitions, 77–8

reasons for takeover
  and management, 123
  and PR, 108, 113, 119
redundancies, 97
regulation, 75–6, 117, 148
relatedness of managerial task, 136–8
Restrictive Trade Practices Act 1976, 172
risk minimisation, 132–42
  added value, 139–40
  common mistakes, 134–5
  cross-border acquisitions, 140–2
  geographical and psychological distance,
    133–4

horizontal, vertical and conglomerate
  acquisitions, 132–3
human factor, 138–9
relatedness, 136–8
Rowntree Mackintosh, xiii
Rumelt, Richard P., 132–3

sales staff, 18
Sandler, Ron, x–xi, 1–15
savings-related share option schemes, 101–2
Schlumberger, 137
share incentive schemes, 100–2
  executive share option, 101
  profit-sharing, 100–1
  savings-related share option, 101–2
shares, and financing acquisitions, 44
Sharpes, 49
Social Security Act 1986, 87, 88, 96
spokesperson, 107
Stallibrass, Michael J.D., xi, 16–28
State Earnings Related Pension Scheme
  (SERPS), 87–8
Stauffer Chemical Company, 58
Stock Exchange, 77–8
  and announcement of takeover, 112,
    114–15
strategy, acquisition, 1–15, 47, 141
  need for, 2–5
  negotiation, 68–71
  price, 67–8
  pensions, 95–7
  practical considerations, 13–15
  screening criteria, 12–13
  strategic vision, 5–8
  value creation, 8–12
Substantial Acquisitions of Shares (SARs)
  rules, 78
super-profits approach to valuation, 37–8
Swift, Jonathan, 118
synergy, 10, 14, 47, 50, 140

Takeover Code (City Code on Takeovers
  and Mergers), 78, 167–8
takeovers, *see* acquisition
taxation
  company information, 153–4, 173
  and financing acquisitions, 45
Taylor, Jonathan F., xi, 47–60
team, acquisitions, 17, 146
Textline Abstracts, 143
timing, 16

Tomkins, 135
Trade and Industry, Department of (DTI),
    144
trade practices, and financial valuation, 39
transfer pricing, 104
Treaty of Rome, 172
trusts, pension, 86
'turnarounds', 11, 14, 141, 142

United States of America (USA)
    acquisition mistakes, 135–6
    diversification errors, 135
    Hart–Scott–Rodino Antitrust
        Improvements Act, 75
    junk-bond market, 46
    M&A consultants, 22
    purchase of companies in, xiii, 42, 134,
        141
    value creation performance, 136–7
    warranties, 80

Vahlne, J.E., 134
value
    adding, 50–2, 139–40
    creation, 2–3, 8–12
        US study, 136–7
vertical acquisitions, 133
vision, strategic, 5–8
Vivian, P., 120, 122

warehouse trust, 106
warranties, 80–2
    limitations on, 83
Waterman, Robert H., Jr, 132
Whitworth, 49
Williams Holdings, 135
Wood, Richard, xi–xii, 120–31
Wray, Martin, xii, 107–19

Yellow Book (Rules governing the
        Admission of Securities to Listing),
        78